PREVIOUS BOOKS:

DO '-YOU BELIEVE in '-GOD??? 'IS, '-DESTINY 'REAL???

DWAYNE W. ANDERSON

DO '-YOU BELIEVE IN '-GOD??? 'IS, '-DESTINY 'REAL???

iUniverse books may be ordered through booksellers or by contacting:

iUniverse
1663 Liberty Drive
Bloomington, IN 47403
www.iuniverse.com
844-349-9409

ISBN: 978-1-6632-3649-4 (sc)
ISBN: 978-1-6632-3651-7 (hc)
ISBN: 978-1-6632-3650-0 (e)

Library of Congress Control Number: 2022913908

Print information available on the last page.

iUniverse rev. date: 07/07/2022

WITHOUT a '-DOUBT, OUR LIVES are '-ETCHED; and, '-ARTICULATED in '-TIME' to an '-EVENTUALITY; of '-GOD'S VERY OWN '-PURPOSE, to '-OUR '-VERY '-OWN PURPOSE of '-BEING; in the '-EXISTENCE/EXPANSE of '-TIME!!!~' OUR '-time OF '-LIVES (BIRTHS, DEATHS, MARRIAGES, CHILDREN, etc.); are '-EXACTLY '-SET by '-GOD!!!~' ALREADY '-PROVEN through '-**R**ECIPROCAL-**S**EQUENCING-**N**UMEROLOGY-**RSN**; and, **R**ECIPROCAL-**S**EQUENCED-**I**NVERSED-**R**EALITIES-**RSIR**!!!~' AGAIN; ENJOY the '-READS!!!~'

BULLET POINTS FOR: DO '-YOU BELIEVE in '-GOD??? 'IS, '-DESTINY 'REAL???

- *THE LIFE AND DEATH OF CELEBRITIES –*
- *THE LIFE AND DEATH OF SCIENTISTS –*
- *THE LIFE AND DEATH OF COMMON PEOPLE –*
- *INTRASPECTION of GOD, the UNIVERSE; and, the MAN/ WOMAN '-INSIDE –*
- *READING; and, UNDERSTANDING the'- SCIENCE of '-NUMBERS in the FOCUS of Reciprocal-Sequencing-Numerology-RSN-'*
- *DISCOVERER & FOUNDER of RECIPROCAL SEQUENCING INVERSED REALITIES – EQUATIONS of '-REALITY in LIFE & DEATH - AUTHOR: DWAYNE W. ANDERSON -*

I've '-**CREATED** a **NEW TYPE** of **PHILOSOPHY** (**R**eciprocal-**S**equencing-**N**umerology)/ (*Reciprocal-Sequenced-Inversed-Realities*) that '-**PROVES** without '-**QUESTION** the '-**PRESENCE** of **GOD'S EXISTENCE** in our **DAILY AFFAIRS!!!!!~'**

DWAYNE W. ANDERSON

Do `-YOU BELIEVE in `-GOD???'

YOU know WHY there's not ANOTHER PERSON talking about GOD like `-ME!!!~' THAT'S because IT'S not UNVEILED to THEM; or, YOU!!!~' GOD blocks MINDS!!!~' AND, HE can BLOCK yours; and, EVERYONE ELSES; just as WELL!!!~' INITIALLY, HE did IT (BLOCKED) ME; just as WELL!!!~' STUDY the FOLLOWING `-SUBJECTS: ANATOMY, PHYSIOLOGY, BIOLOGY, ETC., etc., ETC. (of ALL of `-GOD'S `-CREATIONS); and, ASK for GOD to REVEAL HIMSELF to YOU!!!~' WHEN `-GOD reveals HIMSELF to YOU, IT is so BLATANTLY `-obvious; about HIS EXISTENCE!!!~' NOTICE the BODY of a UFC FIGHTER; and, NOTE all of its CONTOURS, SENSES; and, ANGLES; with the 60 thousand miles worth of the CARDIOVASCULAR SYSTEM'S TUBULES (VESSELS) (2 ½ times around the WORLD) in (EACH `-BODY), ORGANIZED PERFECTLY; or, YOU'RE `-DEAD!!!~' ALL, from ONE CELL = ALL ORGANS, ALL TISSUES, ALL 37 to 100 TRILLION (DIVERSIFIED) CELLS with SPECIALIZED STRUCTURES (MUSCLE CELLS, included) organized BEAUTIFULLY; PERFECTLY = FROM ONE (`-1) tiny CELL (SPERM/EGG GAMETE = ZYGOTE)!!!~' FROM `-SCRATCH; With EVOLUTION, can ONE tiny CELL design ITS (FUTURE) ANATOMICAL (VARIED) `-STRUCTURES; and, ALL of its CONTOURS at ONE time: a HEART (I could DESCRIBE IT in the SUM of an HOUR SESSION), LIVER, SPLEEN, PANCREAS, KIDNEYS, INTESTINES, STOMACH, LUNGS, BRAIN, LYMPHATIC SYSTEMS, BARORECEPTORS, ETC., etc., ETC./ DNAs/RNAs!!!~' ASK `-GOD to UNVEIL `-HIMSELF; to `-YOU; and, to EVERYONE `-ELSE; just as WELL!!!~' OUR `-ABILITIES are DIFFERENT from `-GOD'S `-ABILITIES!!!~' They are `-(RECIPROCALS)-' of EACH `-OTHER!!!~' SEE `-GOD'S `-GLORIOUS `-(CREATIONS); and, YOU'LL SEE the `-(LIGHT); as `-IT'S (ALL); in the (SCIENCES)!!!~'-

From:

DWAYNE W. ANDERSON

ON WHO I AM, I `-UNVEIL in MY `-BOOKS!!!~'

(I'm FULLY VACCINATED; and, BOOSTED)!!!~'

AT&T COLLEAGUES /|\ DEATHS of CO-WORKERS /|\ !!!~'

BARBARA JEAN WINSTON = (50) = AGE Of DEATH!!!~'
(DON'T KNOW CAUSE of DEATH)

BORN = 2/14/1963 = 2 + 14 + 19 + 63 = (98) = BIRTH/DAY #
`-NUMBER!!!~'

BIRTH/YEAR = (63) = ("FLIP EVERY "6" OVER to a "9"); ("FLIP
EVERY "3" OVER to a "8") = (98)

98 + 98 = 196 = (96 x 1) = 96 = RECIPROCAL = (69)

(98) = 9 + 8 = 17

BIRTH FRAG # = 2 + 1 + 4 + 1 + 9 + 6 + 3 = (26) = "DAY of DEATH
(26th)"!!!~'

DEATH = 10/26/2013 = 10 + 26 + 20 + 13 = (69) = DEATH/DAY
# `-NUMBER!!!~'

(69) = 6 + 9 = (15) = 17 + 15 = (32)!!!~'

DWAYNE W. ANDERSON

DEATH FRAG # = 1 + 0 + 2 + 6 + 2 + 0 + 1 + 3 = (15)!!!~'

BIRTH/DAY-to-DEATH/DAY = 111 DAYS = AGES of DEATH = 50 + 61 = 111

365 (-) 111 = 254 = (2 + 5 + 4) = 11

BIRTH = (2/14) = 2 + 14 = 16

DEATH = (10/26) = 26 (-) 10 = 16

DEATH/DAY = (10/26) = 10 + 26 = 36 = RECIPROCAL = (63)

BIRTH/YEAR = (63)

KIM COLLINS HARVEY = (61) = AGE Of DEATH!!!~' (LONG FIGHT with CANCER)

BORN = 11/25/1958 = 11 + 25 + 19 + 58 = (113) = BIRTH/DAY # '-NUMBER!!!~'

(113) = 11 x 3 = (33)

(113) = 13 x 1 = (13) / BIRTH/YEAR = (58) = 5 + 8 = (13)

BIRTH/FRAG # = 1 + 1 + 2 + 5 + 1 + 9 + 5 + 8 = (32)!!!~'

(32) = (8 x 4) = (84) = RECIPROCAL = (48)

DEATH = 6/30/2020 = 6 + 30 + 20 + 20 = (76) = DEATH/DAY # '-NUMBER!!!~'

(76) = (7 + 6) = (13)

- 4 -

DEATH FRAG # = 6 + 3 + 0 + 2 + 0 + 2 + 0 = (13)!!!~'

BIRTH-to-DEATH = 217 DAYS = (2 + 1 + 7) = (10)

365 (-) 217 = (148) = (1 + 4 + 8) = (13)

(10 + 13) = (23) = RECIPROCAL = (32)

DEATH/DAY = (6/30) = 63 + 0 = 63 = RECIPROCAL = (36)

BIRTH/DAY = (11/25) = 11 + 25 = (36)

(36) = RECIPROCAL (INVERSE/REALITY) = (63)!!!~'

(EXCERPT from MY LATEST MOST RECENT BOOK):

DEATH CIPHERS/CYPHERS OF LIFE & DEATH!!!~' To be Certain there are Patterns in OUR LIVES & OUR DEATHS!~' Patterns so obvious that the Mind cannot Escape Them!~' These Patterns lead down a Narrow Path to an Awakening of an Understanding that will Illuminate Mankind's Existence for the Rest of GOD's Current Creation's Existence of Time!!!~' This Book Unlocks the PATTERNS and FORMULAS to All of these Eventualities with their '-CERTAINTIES '-INDEED of these '-LIFE/DEATH ('-PENDULUM '-FLOW '-CALCULATIONS) with and of ('-TIME) that comes along with the Help of Aids from My Previous ('-3) /|\ ('-3) Books in Series of the REAL PROPHET of DOOM (Dwayne W. Anderson)!!!~' Enjoy the READS!!!~'

(DWAYNE W ANDERSON) AUTHOR - Retired Site Infrastructure Senior Engineer/Integrated Planner in Telecommunications. Former California licensed LIFE, HEALTH; AND, DISABILITY INSURANCE

AGENT. A retired FOREMAN in the CONSTRUCTION INDUSTRY. Certified in MEDIATION/ARBITRATION from the UNIVERSITY of BERKELEY, in CALIFORNIA. Singer, Songwriter, Musician, Prophet; and, Author!!!~'

CIVIL RIGHTS ACTIVIST VERNON EULION JORDAN, JR. was BORN on (8/15/1935)!~' (8/15) = (85 x 1) = (`-85) = AGE of `-DEATH for VERNON!~' BIRTH/YEAR = (`-35) = "FLIP EVERY (`-3) OVER to an (`-8)" = (`-85) = `-HIS very OWN AGE of `-DEATH!~' DEATH = 3/1/2021 = (8x1) (2+0+2+1) = (`-85)!~

BROADCASTER ROGER MUDD `-DIED on (3/9) = RECIPROCAL = (93) = AGE of DEATH for ROGER!~' `BIRTHDAY # `-NUMBER = (2+9+19+28) = (58) = "FLIP EVERY (3) OVER to an (8)" = (53) = `DEATH/DAY # `-NUMBER = (3+9+20+21) = (`-53) = 3(9's)!~' DIED (28) DAYS after BIRTHDAY & was BORN in (28)!~'

PERFORMER JACK SHELDON DIED on (12/27/2019)!~' BORN on (11+30+19+31) = 91 = RECIPROCAL = 19 = DIED in the YEAR of 19!~' BIRTH/YEAR = 1931 = (93x1x1) = 93 = RECIPROCAL = 39 = DEATH/YEAR = 20+19 = 39 = DEATH/DAY = (12+27) = 39!~' DIED 338 DAYS from BIRTHDAY = 888 = DIED at AGE 88!~

PERFORMER JACK SHELDON was BORN (1+1+3+0+1+9+3+1) = (`-19) = DIED in the YEAR of 19!~' DIED on (1+2+2+7+2+0+1+9) = (`-24)!~ (19/24) = (1-9) (2x4) = 88 = AGE of DEATH for JACK SHELDON!~ BIRTH/YEAR = 1931 = "FLIP EVERY (3) OVER to an (8)" = (1-9) (8x1) = 88 = AGE of DEATH for JACK!

FRENCH DANCER PATRICK DUPOND DIED on (3/5) in (20+21=41) and was BORN on (3/14) = (3)(1 + 4) = (35) = BIRTH/DAY = DEATH/DAY!~' MARVELOUS MARVIN HAGLER DIED on (3/13) = (33 x 1) = (33) and was BORN on (5/23) = (5(-)2) (3) = (33)!~' (33 + 33) = (66) = AGE of DEATH for MR. HAGLER!~'

ELGIN BAYLOR DIED at the AGE of 86 TODAY!~' BIRTHDAY = 9+16+19+34 = 78!~' ELGIN DIED 178 DAYS before HIS NEXT BIRTH/DAY!~' 365 (-) 178 = 187 = 87 (-) 1 = 86 = AGE of DEATH for MR. BAYLOR!~' BORN in the YEAR of 34 and DIED on 3/22 = 3 (2 + 2) = 34!~' 1934 = 1 (-) 9 / 3 + 4 = 87!~'

ELGIN BAYLOR DIED at the AGE of 86 TODAY!~' HE was BORN in the YEAR of 34 and DIED on 3/22 = 3 (2 + 2) = 34!~' (34 + 34) = 68 = RECIPROCAL = 86 = AGE of DEATH for ELGIN BAYLOR!~' DIED on 3 + 22 + 20 + 21 = 66!~' FLIP ONE (6) OVER to a (9) = 9/6 = BORN on 9/16 = 9 (-) 1 (6) = 86!~

ELGIN BAYLOR DIED at the AGE of 86 TODAY!~' BIRTH/DAY = 9/16 = 16 (-) 9 = 7!~' DEATH/DAY = 3/22 = 22 (-) 3 = 19!~' (7/19) = (7 + 1) 9 = 89 = "FLIP EVERY (9) OVER to a (6)" = 86 = AGE of DEATH for MR. ELGIN BAYLOR!~' BIRTH/DAY = 9/16 = 9+16 = 25!~' DEATH/DAY = 3/22 = 3+22 = 25!~"

ACTOR GEORGE SEGAL DIED YESTERDAY at the AGE of 87!~' BIRTH/DAY # = 2+13+19+34 = 68!~' DEATH/DAY # = 3+23+20+21 = 67!~' BIRTH/DAY = 2/13 = (23x1) = 23 = DAY of DEATH = 23rd!~' FRAGMENTED BIRTH/DAY # = 2+1+3+1+9+3+4 = 23 = DAY of DEATH!~' FRAGMENTED DEATH/DAY # = 3+2+3+2+0+2+1 = 13 = DAY of BIRTH = 13th!~'

GEORGE SEGAL DIED at the AGE of 87!~' BIRTH/YEAR = 1934 = (1-9) (3+4) = 87 = AGE/DEATH!~' BIRTH = 2+13+19+34 = 68!~' DEATH = 3+23+20+21 = 67!~' 6(8)/6(7) = MINUS the 6's = 87 = AGE/DEATH!~' BIRTH = 2/13 = RECIPROCAL = 31/2 = 3 to 8 / 2 to 7 = 81/7 = 87 x 1 = 87 = AGE/DEATH = 32 = RECIPROCAL = 23 = DAY of DEATH = 2/13 = DAY of BIRTH!~'

CHILDREN'S AUTHOR BEVERLY CLEARY DIED at the AGE of 104!~' BIRTH = 4+12+19+16 = 51!~' DEATH = 3+25+20+21 = 69 = 6+9 = 15 DEATH = RECIPROCAL = 51 = BIRTH!~' BIRTH/DAY = 4/12 = 41 x 2 = DEATH/YEAR = 20+21 = 41!~' DEATH/DAY = 3/25 = 35 x 2 = BIRTH/YEAR = 19+16 = 35!~' DEATH/YEAR = 20/21 = (2 + 2) 01 = 401 = RECIPROCAL = 104 = AGE of DEATH!~'

QUEEN ELIZABETH II had HER entire LIFE in HER BIRTH/DAY = 4/21/19/26!~' MARRIED at 21!~' PRINCE PHILIP MARRIED at 26 = RECIPROCAL = 62 = DAYS in DEATH from BIRTHDAY!~' WHAT'S LEFT? 4/19 = 49 x 1 = 49 = DAY PRINCE PHILIP DIES = RECIPROCAL = 94 = HER AGE at the TIME of HIS DEATH!~'

HUMANS DILIGENTLY work on ONE TASK at a TIME; while, GOD is OUR '-RECIPROCAL-'; as to WHERE HE works INDUSTRIOUSLY on EVERYTHING (ALL THINGS = ATOMS, CELLS) at the SAME TIME SIMULTANEOUSLY!!!~' TO DESCRIBE GOD, HE is the (END-ALL-BE-ALL) of INTELLIGENCE, TIMING; and, POWER!!!~'

49'er GREG CLARK dies at the AGE of 49

DEATH/DAY = 7/7 = 7 x 7 = 49

FRAGMENTED BIRTHDAY # = 4 + 7 + 1 + 9 + 7 + 2 = 30

FRAGMENTED DEATHDAY # = 7 + 7 + 2 + 0 + 2 + 1 = 19

30 + 19 = 49

BIRTH/YEAR = 1972 = 19 + 72 = 91 = RECIPROCAL = 19 = FRAGMENTED DEATHDAY # -

TIME from BIRTH to DEATH = 91 DAYS = BIRTH/YEAR = 19 + 72 = 91 = RECIPROCAL = 19 = FRAGMENTED DEATHDAY # -

BIRTHDAY # = 4 + 7 + 19 + 72 = 102

DEATHDAY # = 7 + 7 + 20 + 21 = 55

102 - 55 = 47 = BIRTH/DAY -

BIRTH/YEAR = 72 = "FLIP EVERY ('-2) OVER to a ('-7)" = 77 = HIS DEATH/DAY -

CALENDAR YEAR = 365 - 91 = 274 = RECIPROCAL = 472 = BIRTH/DAY & YEAR of BIRTH = 47 + 2 = 49!!!~' (4/7/19/72) = EVERY DETAIL of HIS DEATH was in HIS BIRTH/DAY!!!~'

JACQUELINE KENNEDY ONASSIS died on 5/19 which was (70) days away from BIRTH to DEATH!~' CALENDAR YEAR = 365 - 70 = (295)!~' JOHN F. KENNEDY was BORN on (5/29) = SWIPE TWO = 295!~' JFK'S birthday # = 5 + 29 + 19 + 17 = (70)!~' HUSBAND & WIFE (LINKED TOGETHER) in BIRTH & DEATH!!!~'

NIKOLA TESLA (SERBIAN-AMERICAN INVENTOR, ELECTRICAL/MECHANICAL ENGINEER; &, FUTURIST of (AC = ALTERNATING CURRENT) had a BIRTHDAY of (7/10) = 7 + 10 = 17 = HIS DEATHDAY (JAN. 7TH)!!!~' AMERICAN ACTOR MARK BLUM was BORN in 1950 = 19 + 50 = 69 = HIS AGE of DEATH!!!~' 6 x 9 = 54 = HIS BIRTHDAY 5/14!!!~'

AMERICAN INVENTOR RON POPEIL died on 7/28 = 7 + 28 = 35 = was BORN in 35 = RECIPROCAL = 53 = BIRTHDAY!~' From BIRTH-to-DEATH = 86 days & DIES at the AGE of 86!~' AMERICAN POLITICIAN RAYMOND J. DONOVAN from BIRTH-to-DEATH = 90 days & DIES at the AGE of 90!!!~' A UNIVERSAL PATTERN!

BOUTROS BOUTROS-GHALI (FORMER SECRETARY-GENERAL of the UNITED NATIONS) BIRTHDAY = 11/14 =

11x14 = 154 = DEATHDAY # NUMBER = 2+16+20+16 = 54!~'
BIRTH = 11+14+19+22 = 66 = 6x6 = 36!~' DEATH/YEAR = 2016
= 20+16 = 36 = RECIPROCAL = 63 = FLIP EVERY 6 over to a 9 =
93 = AGE of DEATH!~' From BIRTH-to-DEATH = 94 days = 9 x
4 = 36!~'

BASEBALL'S LOU BROCK'S BIRTHDAY = 6/18 = 6x18 = 108 =
RECIPROCAL = 801 = 80+1 = 81!~' From BIRTH-to-DEATH = 80
days & DIES at the AGE of 81!~' DEATH/DAY = 9/6 = 9x6 = 54x2
= 108!~' AMERICAN ACTRESS ANNE FRANCIS from BIRTH-
to-DEATH = 108 days & DIES at the AGE of 80!~' BIRTH = 9/16 =
9x16 = 144 = 1+4(4) = 54x2 = 108!~'

41st U.S. PRESIDENT GEORGE H. W. BUSH was BORN in 1924
= 2(194) = from BIRTH-to-DEATH = 194 days = 94x1 & = DIES at
the AGE of 94 = 9x4 = 36!~' WIFE FIRST LADY BARBARA BUSH
DIED at 92 & was BORN on 6/8 & DIED on 4/17 = 4x17 = 68!~'
68+68 = 136 = RECIP = 631 = 63+1 = 64 = FLIP 6-to-9 = 94!!!~'
BORN in 1(92)5 = 92(-)51 = 41!~'

LEGENDARY FLORIDA STATE COACH BOBBY BOWDEN died
TODAY at the AGE of 91!~' BIRTH = 11/8 = 11x8 = 88 = DIES on
8/8 just like COUNTRY MUSIC STAR GLEN CAMPBELL was
BORN on 4/22 = 4x22 = 88 & HE too DIED on 8/8!!!~' BORN in
29 = RECIP = 92 & DIES 92 days from BIRTH-TO-DEATH in the
YEAR of HIS 92ND BIRTHDAY!!!~'

KOOL & the GANG's SAXOPHONIST DENNIS D.T. THOMAS
died & was BORN in 1951 = 19+51 = 70 = HIS very OWN AGE of
DEATH!~' ACTOR MARK BLUM was BORN in 1950 = 19+50
= 69 = HIS very OWN AGE of DEATH!~' POINTER SISTERS
BONNIE POINTER was BORN in 1950 = 19+50 = 69 = HER very
OWN AGE of DEATH!!!~'

ACTRESS MICHELLE DORIS THOMAS (FATHER was DENNIS D.T. THOMAS) was BORN on a 23RD & DIED on a 23RD!~' SHE was BORN in 68 = FLIP EVERY 6 over to a 9 = 98 & DIED in the YEAR of 98!~' WAS BORN in SEPTEMBER (9) & DIED in DECEMBER (12) = RECIPROCAL = (21) = 21+9 = 30 = HER AGE of DEATH!!!~'

AMERICAN ACTRESS JANE WITHERS died on 8/7/2021!~' 8x7 = 56!~' 8+7+20+21=56!~' 56 = RECIPROCAL = 65 = FLIP EVERY 6 over to a 9 = 95 = AGE of DEATH!~' BIRTH = 4+12+19+26 = 61!~' 61+56 = 117 & DIED 117 DAYS from BIRTH-to-DEATH!~' FRAG BIRTH # = 25 / FRAG DEATH # = 20!~' 25+20 = 45 = 9x5 = 95 = AGE of DEATH!!!~'

DONALD HENRY RUMSFELD died within what would have been HIS 67th Year of being MARRIED!~' (67=RECIP=76) BIRTH = 7+9+19+32 = 67!~' DEATH = 6+29+20+21 = 76!~' BIRTHDAY = 7/9 = RECIP = 9/7 = FLIP 9 OVER to a 6 = 6/7!~' DEATH/DAY = 6/29 = 6(2(-)9) = 67!~' DEATH/DAY = 6/29 = 6+29 = 35 = RECIP = 53 = FRAG BIRTH&DEATH DAYS ADDED UP TOGETHER!~' DIED 355 DAYS from BIRTH-to-DEATH!!!~'

DONALD RUMSFELD (AMERICAN POLITICIAN) 67/76 on BIRTH#/death# '-NUMBERS!~' 76/67 on birth#/DEATH# = EMMANUEL N'DJOKE "MANU" DiBANGO (CAMEROONIAN MUSICIAN) & CHARLES MILLES MANSON (AMERICAN CRIMINAL & CULT LEADER)!~' ACTRESS NANCY KULP (THE BEVERLY HILLBILLIES) BIRTH# = 76 & DEATH# in REVERSE = 67!!!~'

TODAY SHOW WEATHERMAN WILLARD SCOTT died at the AGE of 87!~' BIRTHDAY = 3/7 = FLIP 3's TO 8's = 87!~' BIRTH YEAR = 1934 = (1-9)(3+4) = 87!~' BIRTHDAY # NUMBER = 3+7+19+34 = 63 = RECIPROCAL = 36 = (9x4) = DEATHDAY =

9/4!!!~' This PATTERN was DOCUMENTED over 100 TIMES in MY ten BOOKS!!!~'

AMERICAN ACTOR MICHAEL K. WILLIAMS died on 9/6 = 9x6 = 54!~' HE died 77 DAYS from BIRTH-to-DEATH = 77x2 = 154!~' HE died at the AGE of 54!~' BIRTHYEAR = 1966 = (1+9)66 = 66(-)10 = 56 = HIS death/day # = 9+6+20+21 = 56!~' BIRTH/YEAR = 66 = FLIP 6 over to a 9 = 9/6!!!~' DEATH PATTERN!!!~'

AMERICAN ACTOR MICHAEL K. WILLIAMS died on 9/6 = 9x6 = 54!~' HE died at the AGE of 54!~' BIRTH/YEAR = 1966 = (1+9)66 = 66(-)10 = 56 = HIS death/day # = 9+6+20+21 = 56!~' FRAGMENTED BIRTH/DAY # = 1+1+2+2+1+9+6+6 = 28x2 = 56!~' FRAGMENTED DEATH/DAY # = 9+6+2+0+2+1 = 20 = (5x4)!!!~'

COMEDIAN/ACTOR NORM MACDONALD dies at the AGE of 61!~' BIRTHDAY = 10/17!~' 17 =RECIP= 71!~' 71(-)10 = 61 = AGE of DEATH!~' DEATHDAY = 9/14 = 9x14 = 126 =RECIP= 621 = 62(-)1 = 61!~' 9+1+4+2+0+2+1 = 19 =RECIP= 91 = FLIP 9 to 6 = 61!~' SEPT has 30 days = 30(-)14 = 16 =RECIP= 61!!!~'

COMEDIAN/ACTOR NORM MACDONALD dies at the AGE of 61!~' FRAGMENTED BIRTHDAY # NUMBER = 1+0+1+7+1+9+5+9 = 33 = DIED this MANY days FROM birth-TO-death = 33!~' 365(-)33 = 332 = 33xtimes2!~' BIRTHDAY # = 105/DEATHDAY # = 64!~' 105+64= 169 =RECIP= 961 = MONTH (9) & AGE of DEATH (61)!!!~'

ANTHONY AJ JOHNSON was BORN on 5/5 and DIED at the AGE of 55 just like TAMMY WYNETTE was BORN on 5/5 and DIED at the AGE of 55!~' IF ANTHONY died at the AGE of 56 = DEATH/DAY '# = 9+6+20+21 = 56 just like TOMMY TINY DEBO LISTER JR. died on 12+10+20+20 = 62 = at the AGE of 62!!!~'

RAPPER/MODEL/JOCKEY CHYNNA MARIE ROGERS BIRTHDAY = 8/19/19/94 = in REVERSE = 94(-)19(-)19(-)8 = 48 = DAY of DEATH = APRIL 8th!~' 7th HEAVEN LORENZO BRINO BIRTH = 9/21/19/98 = FRAG # = 9+2+1+1+9+9+8 = 39 = DAY of DEATH = MARCH 9th!~' BIRTHDAY # = 147 = 14+7 = 21 = AGE of DEATH!!!~'

RAY FOSSE (AMERICAN BASEBALL PLAYER) died at the AGE of 74!!!~' HIS `-BIRTHDAY # `-NUMBER = 4+4+19+47 = 74!!!~' This is a PATTERN of 100 TIMES over in MY 10 BOOKS!!!~' FROM BIRTH-to-DEATH = 173 DAYS = 73 + 1 = 74!!!~' `-BORN in 47 = RECIPROCAL = 74 = `-AGE of `-DEATH!!!~' PATTERN

GENERAL COLIN POWELL died TODAY at the AGE of 84!~' BIRTH/YEAR = 1937 = 1(-)9/3(-)7 = 84!~' DEATH/DAY # = 10 + 18 + 20 + 21 = 69!~' DIED from BIRTH-to-DEATH at 169 DAYS!~' 69 = 6x9 = 54 = RECIPROCAL = 45 = BIRTH/DAY = APRIL 5th!~' 1937 = 37 (-) 19 = 18 = DAY of DEATH!!!~' A MARKED PATTERN of TIME!!!~'

BOB SAGET was BORN on 5/17/1956 = (5)(1-7) = 56 = RECIPROCAL = 65 = AGE of DEATH = RECIPROCAL = 56 = YEAR of BIRTH!~' ROBERT DURST was BORN on 4/12/1943 = 4(1+2) = 43 = YEAR of BIRTH!~' RD BIRTH/DAY # = 4+12+19+43 = 78 = AGE of DEATH!~' VERY COMMON PATTERN OUTLINED in 10 BOOKS!~'

SIDNEY POITIER BIRTH/YEAR = 1927 = 9(7-2-1) = 94 = AGE of DEATH!~' DEATH/DAY = 1+6+20+22 = 49 = RECIPROCAL = 94 = AGE of DEATH!~' FRAGMENTED BIRTH/DAY # = 2+2+0+1+9+2+7 = 23 = A PROPHETIC # `-NUMBER = AS OUTLINED in PREVIOUS 10 BOOKS = RECIPROCAL = 32 = DIED 320 DAYS from BIRTHDAY!!!~'

BETTY WHITE BIRTH/YEAR = 1922 = 9(2-2-1) = 99 = AGE of
DEATH!~' BIRTH/DAY = 1/17 = (1+17) = 18 = DIED 18 DAYS
from BIRTH/DAY = (2x9) = 2(9's) = 99 = AGE of DEATH!~' BETTY
WHITE FRAGMENTED BIRTH/DAY # = 1+1+7+1+9+2+2 = 23!~'
BORN in 1922 = 19+22 = 41 = DEATH/YEAR = 20+21 = 41!!!~'

MUSICAL ARTIST/ACTOR - MEAT LOAF - (MICHAEL LEE
ADAY) was BORN in (47) = RECIPROCAL = (74) = AGE of
DEATH!!!~' RAY FOSSE (AMERICAN BASEBALL PLAYER)
was BORN in (47) & RECIPROCAL = (74) = AGE of DEATH!~'
HIS '-BIRTHDAY # '-NUMBER = 4+4+19+47 = 74!~' This is a
PATTERN in MY 10 '-PREVIOUS BOOKS!!!~'

RONNIE SPECTOR dies at the AGE of 78!!!~' BIRTH = 8/10 /|\
DEATH = 1/12 /|\ "FLIP EVERY ('-2) OVER to a ('-7)" = 1/17 =
RECIPROCAL = 71/1 = (7+1) (1) = 81 = DEATH /|\ BIRTH = 8/10
= (81 + 0) = 81!!!~'

RONNIE SPECTOR died 210 DAYS from BIRTH-TO-DEATH /|\
DEATH = 1/12 = RECIPROCAL = 21/1 = (21 x 1) = 21....210 = (21 + 0)
= 21!!!~' DEATH/YEAR = 20 + 22 = (42) = 21 + 21!!!~' DEATH = 1/12
= RECIPROCAL = 21/1 = 21 + 1 = 22 = DEATH/YEAR = ('-22)!!!~'

RONNIE SPECTOR died 365 (-) 210 = (155) DAYS from BIRTH-
TO-DEATH!!!~' DEATH/DAY # '-NUMBER = 1 + 12 + 20 + 22
= 55 /|\ 155 = (55 x 1) = 55!!!~' (155) = RECIPROCAL = (551)
= (55 + 1) = 56 = (7 x 8) = DIED at the AGE of ('-78) = RONNIE
SPECTOR!!!~'

RONNIE SPECTOR was BORN in the MONTH of ('-8); AND,
DIED in the MONTH of ('-1) = ('-81) = BIRTH/DAY = 8/10 = (8 +
10) = ('-18) = RECIPROCAL = ('-81)!!!~'

RONNIE SPECTOR `-BIRTH/DAY # `-NUMBER = 8 + 10 + 19 + 43 = 80!!!~' BIRTH = 8/10 = (8 x 10) = 80!!!~' BIRTH/YEAR = 1943 = RECIPROCAL = 3491 = (3 + 4) (9 – 1) = (`-78) = AGE of `-DEATH for RONNIE SPECTOR!!!~'

RONNIE SPECTOR `-FRAGMENTED `-BIRTH/DAY # `-NUMBER = 8 + 1 + 0 + 1 + 9 + 4 + 3 = 26 = "FLIP EVERY (`-2) OVER to a (`-7)" = 76!!!~' "FLIP EVERY (`-6) OVER to a (`-9)" = 79!!!~' (76 + 79) = 155 / `-2 = 77.5 = ROUNDED UP = 78 = AGE of DEATH for RONNIE SPECTOR!!!~'

RONNIE SPECTOR was MARRIED to JONATHAN GREENFIED for 40 YEARS SINCE 1982!!!~' SHE was MARRIED to PHIL SPECTOR for 6 YEARS from 1968 TO 1974!!!~' (40 + 6) = 46 / `-2 = (`-23) = "FLIP EVERY (`-2) OVER to a (`-7)"; "FLIP EVERY (`-3) OVER to an (`-8)" = (`-78) = AGE of DEATH for RONNIE SPECTOR!!!~'

ACTOR/COMEDIAN (LOUIS PERRY ANDERSON) died at the AGE of 68!!!~'

BIRTH/DAY # `-NUMBER = 3/24/19/53 = 3 + 24 + 19 + 53 = 99

DEATH/DAY # `-NUMBER = 1/21/20/22 = 1 + 21 + 20 + 22 = 64

(99 + 64) = 163 = (63 x 1) = 63 = "FLIP EVERY (`-3) OVER to an (`-8)" = 68 = AGE of DEATH for ACTOR/COMEDIAN (LOUIS PERRY ANDERSON)!!!~'

BIRTH/YEAR = 1953 = "FLIP EVERY (`-9) OVER to a (`-6)" = 1653 = (1 x 6) (5 + 3) = 68 = AGE of DEATH for ACTOR/COMEDIAN (LOUIS PERRY ANDERSON)!!!~'

BIRTH/DAY = 3/24 = RECIPROCAL = 42/3 = "FLIP EVERY (`-3) OVER to an (`-8)" = 42/8 = (4 + 2) (8) = 68 = AGE of DEATH for ACTOR/COMEDIAN (LOUIS PERRY ANDERSON)!!!~'

FROM BIRTH-TO-DEATH = 62 DAYS!!!~' (365 (-) 62) = 303 DAYS from BIRTH-TO-DEATH!!!~' 62/303 = RECIPROCAL = 303/62 = (3 + 0 + 3) (6 + 2) = 68 = AGE of DEATH for ACTOR/COMEDIAN (LOUIS PERRY ANDERSON)!!!~'

`-I can't JUDGE `-ANYTHING!!!~' `-I have to ACCEPT `-ALL that `-GOD has ALLOWED and DONE!!!~'

ESTELLE BENNETT (SISTER of RONNIE SPECTOR) from THE RONETTES died at the AGE of 67!!!~'

BIRTHDAY # `-NUMBER = 7/22/19/41 = 7 + 22 + 19 + 41 = 89 = (8 x 9) = 72 = BORN in the MONTH of (`-7); AND, DIED in the MONTH of (`-2)!!!~'

BIRTHDAY # `-NUMBER = 7/22/19/41 = 7 + 22 + 19 + 41 = 89 = RECIPROCAL = 98 = "FLIP EVERY (`-9) OVER to an (`-6)" = 68 = DIED within HER 68th YEAR of `-EXISTENCE!!!~' Was ACTIVE until (`-68) as a SINGER!!!~'

DEATHDAY # `-NUMBER = 2/11/20/09 = 2 + 11 + 20 + 09 = 42 = (6 X 7) = AGE of DEATH for ESTELLE BENNETT from THE RONETTES!!!~'

DEATH/YEAR = 20/09 = (20 + 09) = 29 = RECIPROCAL = 92 = "FLIP EVERY (`-9) OVER to a (`-6)"; "FLIP EVERY (`-2) OVER to a ('-7)" = 67 = AGE of DEATH for ESTELLE BENNETT from THE RONETTES!!!~'

BIRTHDAY = 7/22 = (7 + 22) = 29 = DEATH/YEAR = 20/09 = (20 + 09) = 29

FRAGMENTED BIRTHDAY # '-NUMBER = 7 + 2 + 2 + 1 + 9 + 4 + 1 = 26 = RECIPROCAL = 62 = "FLIP EVERY ('-2) OVER to a ('-7)" = 67 = AGE of DEATH for ESTELLE BENNETT from THE RONETTES!!!~'

FRAGMENTED DEATHDAY # '-NUMBER = 2 + 1 + 1 + 2 + 0 + 0 + 9 = 15!!!~'

(26 + 15) = 41 = BIRTH/YEAR!!!~'

(1941) = (41 (-) 19) = 22

DAY of '-BIRTH = 22nd = DEATH/DAY = 2/11 = (2 x 11) = 22!!!~'

DIED ('-161) DAYS from BIRTH-TO-DEATH = (61 + 1) = 62 = "FLIP EVERY ('-2) OVER to a ('-7)" = 67 = AGE of DEATH for ESTELLE BENNETT from THE RONETTES!!!~'

(365 (-) 161) = 204 = RECIPROCAL = 402 = (40 + 2) = 42 = DEATH/DAY # '-NUMBER for ESTELLE BENNETT from THE RONETTES!!!~'

ACTOR BILL PAXTON (WILLIAM ARCHIBALD PAXTON) died at the AGE of 61!!!~'

BIRTHDAY # '-NUMBER = 5/17/19/55 = 5 + 17 + 19 + 55 = 96

DEATHDAY # `-NUMBER = 2/25/20/17 = 2 + 25 + 20 + 17 = 64

(96 + 64) = 160 = RECIPROCAL = 061 = (61 + 0) = 61 = AGE of DEATH for ACTOR BILL PAXTON (WILLIAM ARCHIBALD PAXTON)!!!~'

(96 (-) 64) = 32 = "A `-PROPHETIC `-NUMBER"!!!~'

FRAGMENTED BIRTHDAY # `-NUMBER = 5 + 1 + 7 + 1 + 9 + 5 + 5 = 33

(3 x 3) = 9 /|\ (3 + 3) = 6 /|\ 96 = BIRTHDAY # `-NUMBER!!!~'

FRAGMENTED DEATHDAY # `-NUMBER = 2 + 2 + 5 + 2 + 0 + 1 + 7 = 19 = RECIPROCAL = 91 = "FLIP EVERY (`-9) OVER to a (`-6)" = 61 = AGE of DEATH for ACTOR BILL PAXTON (WILLIAM ARCHIBALD PAXTON)!!!~'

BIRTHDAY = 5/17 = (5 + 17) = 22 = "FLIP EVERY (`-2) OVER to a (`-7)" = 27

DEATHDAY = 2/25 = (2 + 25) = 27

(27 + 27) = 54 = (9 X 6) = BIRTHDAY # `-NUMBER!!!~'

BIRTH/YEAR = 1955 = (9) (5 + 5 + 1) = 9(11) = "FLIP EVERY (`-9) OVER to a (`-6)" = 6(11) = 61(1) = (61 x 1) = 61 = AGE of DEATH for ACTOR BILL PAXTON (WILLIAM ARCHIBALD PAXTON)!!!~'

BIRTH/YEAR = 1955 = (1 + 5) (9 – 5) = 64 = DEATHDAY # `-NUMBER!!!~'

(`-284) DAYS from BIRTH-TO-DEATH = (2 – 8) (4) = 64 = DEATHDAY # `-NUMBER!!!~'

WAS BORN in the MONTH of (`-5); AND, DIED in the MONTH of (`-2) = 52

BIRTHDAY = 5/17 = "FLIP EVERY (`-7) OVER to a (`-2)" = 5/12 = (52 x 1) = 52

DEATHDAY = 2/25 = RECIPROCAL = 52/2

ACTOR CHRISTOPHER D'OLIER REEVE (MOVIE/SUPERMAN) died at the AGE of 52!!!~'

BIRTH/YEAR = 52 = AGE of DEATH = 52 for ACTOR CHRISTOPHER D'OLIER REEVE (MOVIE/SUPERMAN)!!!~'

DAY of `-BIRTH = 25th = RECIPROCAL = 52 = AGE of DEATH = 52 for ACTOR CHRISTOPHER D'OLIER REEVE (MOVIE/SUPERMAN)!!!~'

BIRTHDAY # `-NUMBER = 9/25/19/52 = 9 + 25 + 19 + 52 = 105 = RECIPROCAL = 501 = (50 + 1) = 51

DEATHDAY # `-NUMBER = 10/10/20/04 = 10 + 10 + 20 + 04 = 44

(105 + 44) = 149 = (14 x 9) = 126 = (1 – 6) (2) = 52 = AGE of DEATH = 52 for ACTOR CHRISTOPHER D'OLIER REEVE (MOVIE/SUPERMAN)!!!~'

(105 (-) 44) = 61 = RECIPROCAL = 16 = (4 X 4) = DEATHDAY # `-NUMBER!!!~'

BIRTHDAY = 9/25 = (25 (-) 9) = 16 = RECIPROCAL = 61

BIRTHDAY = 9/25 = (25 (-) 9) = 16 = (4 X 4) = DEATHDAY # `-NUMBER!!!~'

DIED 15 DAYS from BIRTH-TO-DEATH = BIRTHDAY # `-NUMBER = 105 = (10 + 5) = 15!!!~'

(365 (-) 15) = 350 = (35 + 0) = 35 = (3 x 5) = 15!!!~'

FRAGMENTED BIRTHDAY # `-NUMBER = 9 + 2 + 5 + 1 + 9 + 5 + 2 = 33

FRAGMENTED DEATHDAY # `-NUMBER = 1 + 0 + 1 + 0 + 2 + 0 + 0 + 4 = 8

(33 (-) 8) = 25 = RECIPROCAL = 52 = AGE of DEATH = 52 for ACTOR CHRISTOPHER D'OLIER REEVE (MOVIE/SUPERMAN)!!!~'

MISS USA 2019 (CHESLIE CORRINNE KRYST) died at the AGE of 30!!!~'

BIRTH/DAY # `-NUMBER in `-REVERSE = (91 (-) 19 (-) 28 (-) 4) = 40 = DEATH/DAY = 1/30 = (1 + 3) (0) = 40!!!~'

BIRTHDAY # `-NUMBER = 4/28/19/91 = 4 + 28 + 19 + 91 = 142

DEATHDAY # `-NUMBER = 1/30/20/22 = 1 + 30 + 20 + 22 = 73

(142 + 73) = 215 = (2 x 15) = 30 = AGE of DEATH for MISS USA 2019 (CHESLIE CORRINNE KRYST)!!!~'

(142 (-) 73) = 69 = (6 + 9) = 15 (x 2) = 30 = AGE of DEATH for MISS USA 2019 (CHESLIE CORRINNE KRYST)!!!~'

DAY of DEATH = 30 = AGE of DEATH for MISS USA 2019 (CHESLIE CORRINNE KRYST)!!!~'

FRAGMENTED BIRTHDAY # '-NUMBER = 4 + 2 + 8 + 1 + 9 + 9 + 1 = 34

FRAGMENTED DEATHDAY # '-NUMBER = 1 + 3 + 0 + 2 + 0 + 2 + 2 = 10

(34 + 10) = 44 (x 2) = 88 = DIED this MANY DAYS from BIRTH-TO-DEATH!!!~'

(34 (-) 10) = 24 = BIRTHDAY # '-NUMBER = 142 = RECIPROCAL = 241 = (24 x 1) = 24

BIRTHDAY = 4/28 = (4 + 28) = 32 = "FLIP EVERY ('-2) OVER to a ('-7)" = 37 = RECIPROCAL = 73 = DEATHDAY # '-NUMBER!!!~'

DEATHDAY = 1/30 = (1 x 30) = 30 = AGE of DEATH for MISS USA 2019 (CHESLIE CORRINNE KRYST)!!!~'

BIRTHDAY # NUMBER = 142 = (42 x 1) = 42 = DEATH/YEAR = 20 + 22 = 42

BIRTHDAY # NUMBER = 142 = (14 x 2) = 28 = 2(8's) = 88

('-88) DAYS from BIRTH-TO-DEATH!!!~'

WAS BORN in the MONTH of ('-4); AND, DIED in the MONTH of ('-1) = 41 = (4 (-) 1) = 3 (JUST ADD a ZERO) = 30 = AGE of DEATH for MISS USA 2019 (CHESLIE CORRINNE KRYST)!!!~'

HEIGHT = 5' 6" = (5 x 6) = 30 = AGE of DEATH for MISS USA 2019 (CHESLIE CORRINNE KRYST)!!!~'

DONALD CORTEZ CORNELIUS (SOUL TRAIN) died at the AGE of 75!!!~'

BIRTHDAY # `-NUMBER = 9/27/19/36 = 9 + 27 + 19 + 36 = 91

DEATHDAY # `-NUMBER = 2/1/20/12 = 2 + 1 + 20 + 12 = 35 = (7 X 5) = 75 = AGE of DEATH for DONALD CORTEZ CORNELIUS (SOUL TRAIN)!!!~'

DEATHDAY # `-NUMBER = 2/1/20/12 = 2 + 1 + 20 + 12 = (`-35) = SOUL TRAIN "AIRED" FOR (`-35) YEARS!!!~'

(91 + 35) = 126 = "FLIP EVERY (`-2) OVER to a (`-7)" = 176 = (7) (1 – 6) = 75 = AGE of DEATH for DONALD CORTEZ CORNELIUS (SOUL TRAIN)!!!~'

(91 + 35) = 126 = "FLIP EVERY (`-2) OVER to a (`-7)" = 176 = (76 x 1) = 76 = DIED within HIS 76th YEAR of EXISTENCE!!!~'

(91 (-) 35) = 56 = RECIPROCAL = 65 = HEIGHT = 6' 5"!!!~'

FRAGMENTED BIRTHDAY # `-NUMBER = 9 + 2 + 7 + 1 + 9 + 3 + 6 = 37

FRAGMENTED DEATHDAY # `-NUMBER = 2 + 1 + 2 + 0 + 1 + 2 = 8

(37 + 8) = 45 = (9 x 5) = 95 = "FLIP EVERY (`-9) OVER to a (`-6)" = 65 = HEIGHT = 6' 5"!!!~'

(37 (-) 8) = 29 = RECIPROCAL = 92 = BORN in the MONTH of (`-9); and, DIED in the MONTH of (`-2)!!!~'

BIRTHDAY = (9/2)7 = (27 (-) 9) = 18 = (9 x 2) = BORN in the MONTH of (`-9); and, DIED in the MONTH of (`-2)!!!~'

(`-127) DAYS from BIRTH-TO-DEATH = (1 + 2) (7) = 37 = FRAGMENTED BIRTHDAY # `-NUMBER!!!~'

WAS BORN in the MONTH of (`-9); AND, DIED in the MONTH of (`-2) = 92 = RECIPROCAL = 29 = "FLIP EVERY (`-2) OVER to a (`7)"; "FLIP EVERY (`-9) OVER to a (`-6)" = 76 = DIED within HIS 76th YEAR of EXISTENCE!!!~'

WAS BORN in the MONTH of (`-9); AND, DIED in the MONTH of (`-2) = BIRTHDAY # `-NUMBER = 91 with (`-92) being `-NEXT!!!~'

BIRTHDAY = (9/2)7 = (9 + 27) = 36 = BIRTH/YEAR!!!~'

DEATHDAY = 2/1 = RECIPROCAL = 1/2 = DEATH/YEAR!!!~'

MARRIED to VICTORIA CORNELIUS from (2001 TO 2009)!!!~'

2001 = 2/1/00 = DEATH/DAY!!!~'

2009 = 2/9/00 = RECIPROCAL = 00/9/2 = BORN in the MONTH of (`-9); and, DIED in the MONTH of (`-2)!!!~'

BIRTH/DAY = (9/2)7!!!~'

COMEDIAN/ACTOR RICHARD FRANKLIN LENNOX THOMAS PRYOR SR. died at the AGE of 65!!!~'

BIRTHDAY # `-NUMBER = 12/1/19/40 = 12 + 1 + 19 + 40 = 72

DEATHDAY # `-NUMBER = 12/10/2005 = 12 + 10 + 20 + 05 = 47

BIRTHDAY = 12/1

DEATHDAY = 12/10 = JUST DROP the ZERO = 12/1

BIRTH/YEAR = 1940 = (19 + 40) = 59 = RECIPROCAL = 95 = "FLIP EVERY ('-9) OVER to a ('-6)" = 65 = AGE of DEATH for COMEDIAN/ACTOR RICHARD FRANKLIN LENNOX THOMAS PRYOR SR.!!!~'

BIRTH/YEAR = (1940) = (40 (-) 19) = 21 = RECIPROCAL = 12 = BIRTHDAY & DEATHDAY!!!~'

DEATH/YEAR = 20/05 = "FLIP EVERY ('-2) OVER to a ('-7)" = 70/05 = (70 (-) 05) = 65 = AGE of DEATH for COMEDIAN/ACTOR RICHARD FRANKLIN LENNOX THOMAS PRYOR SR.!!!~'

DEATH/YEAR = (2005) = (20 + 05) = 25 = (72 (-) 47) = 25!!!~'

FROM BIRTH-TO-DEATH there were 9 DAYS!!!~'

(365 (-) 9) = 356 = RECIPROCAL = 653 = (65 x 3) = 195 = (95 x 1) = 95 = "FLIP EVERY ('-9) OVER to a ('-6)" = 65 = AGE of DEATH for COMEDIAN/ACTOR RICHARD FRANKLIN LENNOX THOMAS PRYOR SR.!!!~'

COMEDIAN/ACTOR GENE WILDER (JEROME SILBERMAN) died at the AGE of 83!!!~'

BIRTHDAY # '-NUMBER = 6/11/19/33 = 6 + 11 + 19 + 33 = 69

DEATHDAY # '-NUMBER = 8/29/20/16 = 8 + 29 + 20 + 16 = 73

BIRTH/YEAR = 33 = "FLIP EVERY ('-3) to an ('-8)" = 83 = AGE

of DEATH for COMEDIAN/ACTOR GENE WILDER (JEROME SILBERMAN)!!!~'

REMAINDER = 6 + 11 + 19 = 36 = DEATH/YEAR = (20 + 16) = 36

DEATH/DAY = 8/29 = (8 (-) 2) (9) = 69 = BIRTHDAY # `-NUMBER!!!~'

FROM BIRTH-TO-DEATH there were 79 DAYS = (7 x 9) = 63 = RECIPROCAL = 36!!!~'

(365 (-) 79) = 286 = (2 (-) 8) (6) = 66 = "FLIP EVERY (`-6) OVER to a (`-9)" = 69 = BIRTHDAY # `-NUMBER!!!~'

(365 (-) 79) = 286 = (8) (2 + 6) = 88 = "FLIP EVERY (`-8) OVER to a (`-3)" = 83 = AGE of DEATH for COMEDIAN/ACTOR GENE WILDER (JEROME SILBERMAN)!!!~'

BIRTHDAY = 6/11 /|\ DEATHDAY = 8/29

(6 + 11 + 8 + 29) = 54 = (6 X 9) = BIRTHDAY # `-NUMBER!!!~'

COMEDIAN/ACTOR PAUL MOONEY (PAUL GLADNEY) died at the AGE of 79!!!~'

BIRTHDAY # `-NUMBER = 8/4/19/41 = 8 + 4 + 19 + 41 = 72

DEATHDAY # `-NUMBER = 5/19/20/21 = 5 + 19 + 20 + 21 = 65

BIRTH/YEAR = 41

DEATH/YEAR = 20 + 21 = 41

BIRTH/YEAR = 19/41 = (19 + 41) = 60

PART of DEATH/YEAR = (19 + 20 + 21) = 60

WHAT'S `-LEFT = 8/4/5 = (84 (-) 5) = 79 = AGE of DEATH for COMEDIAN/ACTOR PAUL MOONEY (PAUL GLADNEY)!!!~'

BIRTH/DAY = 8/4 = (8 x 4) = 32 /|\ DEATH/DAY = 5/19 = (5 x 19) = 95

(95 (-) 32) = 63 = (7 X 9) = AGE of DEATH for COMEDIAN/ACTOR PAUL MOONEY (PAUL GLADNEY)!!!~'

BIRTHDAY = 8/4 = (8 + 4) = 12 (x 2) = 24

DEATHDAY = 5/19 = (5 + 19) = 24

(24 + 24) = 48 = RECIPROCAL = 8/4 = BIRTHDAY!!!~'

BIRTH/YEAR = 19/41 = (41 (-) 19) = 22 = "FLIP EVERY (`-2) OVER to a (`-7) = 77!!!~'

FROM BIRTH-TO-DEATH there were 77 DAYS = "FLIP EVERY (`-7) OVER to a (`-2)" = 72 = BIRTHDAY # `-NUMBER!!!~'

FRAGMENTED BIRTHDAY # `-NUMBER = 8 + 4 + 1 + 9 + 4 + 1 = 27 = RECIPROCAL = 72 = BIRTHDAY # `-NUMBER!!!~'

(365 (-) 77) = 288 = (28 + 8) = 36 = RECIPROCAL = 63 = (7 X 9) = AGE of DEATH for COMEDIAN/ACTOR PAUL MOONEY (PAUL GLADNEY)!!!~'

ACTRESS/COMEDIAN JACKIE "MOMS" MABLEY (LORETTA MARY AIKEN) died at the AGE of 81!!!~

BIRTHDAY # `-NUMBER = 3/19/18/94 = 3 + 19 + 18 + 94 = 134

DEATHDAY # `-NUMBER = 5/23/19/75 = 5 + 23 + 19 + 75 = 122

BIRTHDAY # `-NUMBER = 134 = (34 + 1) = 35 = WAS `-BORN in the `-MONTH of (`-3); AND, `-DIED in the `-MONTH of (`-5)!!!~'

BIRTHDAY # `-NUMBER = 134 = (34 + 1) = 35 = (7 X 5) = DEATH/ YEAR!!!~'

BIRTH/DAY = 3/19 = (3 + 19) = 22 = DEATHDAY # `-NUMBER = 122 = (22 x 1) = 22

(22 + 22) = 44 = BIRTHDAY # `-NUMBER = 134 = (1 + 3) (4) = 44

(44 + 44) = 88 = (8 x 11) = (81 x 1) = 81 = AGE of DEATH for ACTRESS/COMEDIAN JACKIE "MOMS" MABLEY (LORETTA MARY AIKEN)!!!~'

BIRTHDAY = 3/19 = RECIPROCAL = 91/3 = (91 (-) 3) = 88

BIRTH/DAY = 3/19 = PART of DEATH/DAY # `-NUMBER = 3/19

WHAT'S LEFT from DEATH/DAY # `-NUMBER = 5/2 /|\ 75 = "FLIP EVERY (`-2) OVER to a (`-7)" = 5/7 /|\ 75 !!!~' (`-RECIPROCALS-')...!!!

BIRTHDAY # `-NUMBER = 134 = (13 x 4) = 52 = FIRST PART of DEATH/DAY!!!~'

(134 + 122) = 256 = (25 + 6) = 31 = "FLIP EVERY (`-3) OVER to an (`-8)" = 81 = AGE of DEATH for ACTRESS/COMEDIAN JACKIE "MOMS" MABLEY (LORETTA MARY AIKEN)!!!~'

BIRTH/YEAR = 94

DEATH/YEAR = 19/75 = (19 + 75) = 94

(94) = (9 x 4) = 36 = (3 x 6) = 18 = RECIPROCAL = 81 = AGE of DEATH for ACTRESS/COMEDIAN JACKIE "MOMS" MABLEY (LORETTA MARY AIKEN)!!!~'

BIRTH/DAY = 3/19 = (3 x 19) = 57 = RECIPROCAL = 75 = DEATH/YEAR!!!~'

DEATH/DAY = 5/23 = (5 (-) 23) = 18 = RECIPROCAL = 81 = AGE of DEATH for ACTRESS/COMEDIAN JACKIE "MOMS" MABLEY (LORETTA MARY AIKEN)!!!~'

BIRTH/YEAR = 18/94 = (94 (-) 18) = 76 = (7 + 6) = 13 = RECIPROCAL = 31 = "FLIP EVERY (`-3) OVER to an (`-8)" = 81 = AGE of DEATH for ACTRESS/COMEDIAN JACKIE "MOMS" MABLEY (LORETTA MARY AIKEN)!!!~'

DEATH/YEAR = 19/75 = (75 (-) 19) = 56 = RECIPROCAL = 65!!!~'

FROM BIRTH-TO-DEATH there were 65 DAYS in TOTAL = (6 x 5) = 30

(365 (-) 65) = 300 = (30 + 0) = 30

FRAGMENTED DEATHDAY # `-NUMBER = 5 + 2 + 3 + 1 + 9 + 7 + 5 = 32 = "A PROPHETIC # `-NUMBER"!!!~'

ACTOR HOWARD HESSEMAN died at the AGE of 81!!!~'

BIRTHDAY # `-NUMBER = 2/27/19/40 = 2 + 27 + 19 + 40 = 88

DEATHDAY # `-NUMBER = 1/29/20/22 = 1 + 29 + 20 + 22 = 72

DEATHDAY = 1/29 = (29 (-) 1) = 28 = 2(8's) = 88 = BIRTHDAY # '-NUMBER!!!~'

BIRTHDAY # '-NUMBER = 88 = (8 x 11) = (81 x 1) = 81 = AGE of DEATH for ACTOR HOWARD HESSEMAN!!!~'

BIRTHDAY = 2/27 = (2 + 27) = 29 = DAY of DEATH!!!~'

HOWARD HESSMAN died on the 29th of the MONTH ('-29) DAYS from BIRTH-TO-DEATH!!!~'

(365 (-) 29) = 336 = (33 (-) 6) = 27 = RECIPROCAL = 72 = DEATHDAY # '-NUMBER!!!~'

FRAGMENTED DEATHDAY # '-NUMBER = 1 + 2 + 9 + 2 + 0 + 2 + 2 = 18 = RECIPROCAL = 81 = AGE of DEATH for ACTOR HOWARD HESSEMAN!!!~'

WAS '-MARRIED to CAROLINE DUCROCQ from 1989-to-2022 = 33 YEARS = "FLIP EVERY ('-3) OVER to an ('-8)" = 88 = BIRTHDAY # '-NUMBER!!!~'

DEATHDAY # '-NUMBER = 72 = (8 X 9) = MARRIED!!!~'

WAS '-MARRIED to CATHERINE MAISON from 1965-to-1974 = 9 (x 2) = 18 = RECIPROCAL = 81 = AGE of DEATH for ACTOR HOWARD HESSEMAN!!!~'

YEARS '-MARRIED = (33 + 9) = 42 = DEATH/YEAR = (20 + 22) = 42

BIRTH/YEAR = 19/40 = (19 + 40) = 59

BIRTHDAY = 2/27 /|\ DEATHDAY = 1/29

(2 + 27 + 1 + 29) = 59

(59 + 59) = 118 = (11 x 8) = 88 = BIRTHDAY # `-NUMBER!!!~'

(59 + 59) = 118 = RECIPROCAL = 811 = (81 x 1) = 81 = AGE of DEATH for ACTOR HOWARD HESSEMAN!!!~'

ACTOR RONALD EARLE GLASS died at the AGE of 71!!!~'

WAS `-BORN in the `-MONTH of (`-7); AND, `-DIED in the `-MONTH of (`-11) = 7/11 = (71 x 1) = (`-71) = AGE of DEATH for ACTOR RONALD EARLE GLASS!!!~'

BIRTHDAY # `-NUMBER = 7/10/19/45 = 7 + 10 + 19 + 45 = 81

DEATHDAY # `-NUMBER = 11/25/20/16 = 11 + 25 + 20 + 16 = 72 = DIED at the AGE of (`-71)!!!~'

BIRTHDAY = 7/10 = (71 + 0) = 71 = AGE of DEATH for ACTOR RONALD EARLE GLASS!!!~'

BIRTHDAY = 7/10 = (7 + 10) = 17 = RECIPROCAL = 71 = AGE of DEATH for ACTOR RONALD EARLE GLASS!!!~'

PART of BIRTHDAY # `-NUMBER = (7 + 10 + 19) = 36

DEATH/DAY = 11/25 = (11 + 25) = 36

DEATH/YEAR = 20/16 = (20 + 16) = 36

(36 + 36) = 72 = DEATH/DAY # `-NUMBER!!!~'

(`-36) = (3 x 6) = 18 = RECIPROCAL = 81 = BIRTHDAY # `-NUMBER!!!~'

DEATH/DAY = 11/25 = RECIPROCAL = 52/11 = (52 + 11) = 63 = RECIPROCAL = 36

DEATH/YEAR = 20/16 = RECIPROCAL = 61/02 = (61 + 02) = 63 = RECIPROCAL = 36

DEATH/YEAR = 20/16 = HALF RECIPROCAL = 61/20 = (61 + 20) = 81 = BIRTHDAY # '-NUMBER!!!~'

FROM BIRTH-TO-DEATH there were 138 DAYS!!!~'

('-138) = (13 + 8) = 21 = "FLIP EVERY ('-2) OVER to a ('-7) = 71 = AGE of DEATH for ACTOR RONALD EARLE GLASS!!!~'

(365 (-) 138) = 227 = (22 + 7) = 29 = (2 x 9) = 18 = RECIPROCAL = 81 = BIRTH/DAY # '-NUMBER!!!~'

BIRTH/MONTH = JULY = 31 DAYS!!!~'

(31 (-) 10) - (DAY of BIRTH) = 21 = "FLIP EVERY ('-2) OVER to a ('-7) = 71 = AGE of DEATH for ACTOR RONALD EARLE GLASS!!!~'

ACTRESS/FASHION MODEL FARRAH LENI FAWCETT (CHARLIE'S ANGELS) died at the AGE of 62!!!~'

WAS '-BORN in the '-MONTH of ('-2); AND, '-DIED in the '-MONTH of ('-6) = 26 = RECIPROCAL = 62 = AGE of DEATH for ACTRESS/FASHION MODEL FARRAH LENI FAWCETT (CHARLIE'S ANGELS)!!!~'

BIRTHDAY # '-NUMBER = 2/2/19/47 = 2 + 2 + 19 + 47 = 70

DEATHDAY # `-NUMBER = 6/25/20/09 = 6 + 25 + 20 + 09 = 60

(70 + 60) = 130 = (13 + 0) = 13 = "A VERY PIVOTAL # `-NUMBER"!!!~'

(70/60) = RECIPROCAL = (60/70) = (67 + 0 + 0) = 67 = "FLIP EVERY (`-7) OVER to a (`-2)" = 62 = AGE of DEATH for ACTRESS/ FASHION MODEL FARRAH LENI FAWCETT!!!~'

PART of DEATH/DAY = (6/2)5 = AGE of DEATH for ACTRESS/ FASHION MODEL FARRAH LENI FAWCETT!!!~'

DEATH/DAY = 6/25 = (62 + 5) = 67 = "FLIP EVERY (`-7) OVER to a (`-2)" = 62 = AGE of DEATH for ACTRESS/FASHION MODEL FARRAH LENI FAWCETT!!!~'

FRAGMENTED BIRTHDAY # `-NUMBER = 2 + 2 + 1 + 9 + 4 + 7 = 25 = DAY of DEATH!!!~'

FRAGMENTED DEATHDAY # `-NUMBER = 6 + 2 + 5 + 2 + 0 + 0 + 9 = 24 = RECIPROCAL = 42 = "FLIP EVERY (`-2) OVER to a (`-7)" = 47 = BIRTH/YEAR!!!~'

DEATH/YEAR = 20/09 = (20 + 09) = 29 = RECIPROCAL = 92 = "FLIP EVERY (`-9) OVER to a (`-6)" = 62 = AGE of DEATH for ACTRESS/FASHION MODEL FARRAH LENI FAWCETT!!!~'

BIRTH/YEAR = 19/47 = (9) (7 (-) 4 (-) 1) = 92 = "FLIP EVERY (`-9) OVER to a (`-6)" = 62 = AGE of DEATH for ACTRESS/FASHION MODEL FARRAH LENI FAWCETT!!!~'

BIRTH/YEAR = 19/47 = (19 + 47) = 66 = 2(6's) = 26 = RECIPROCAL = 62 = AGE of DEATH for ACTRESS/FASHION MODEL FARRAH LENI FAWCETT!!!~'

BIRTH/MONTH = FEBRUARY = 28!!!~'

(28 (-) 2) - (DAY of BIRTH) = 26 = RECIPROCAL = 62 = AGE of DEATH for ACTRESS/FASHION MODEL FARRAH LENI FAWCETT!!!~'

FROM BIRTH-TO-DEATH there are 143 DAYS = (14 x 3) = 42 = RECIPROCAL = 24 = FRAGMENTED DEATH/DAY # '-NUMBER!!!~'

(365 (-) 143) = 222 /|\ BIRTH/DAY = 2/2

ACTOR DAVID FITZGERALD DOYLE (CHARLIE'S ANGELS) died at the AGE of 67!!!~'

BIRTHDAY # '-NUMBER = 12/1/19/29 = 12 + 1 + 19 + 29 = 61

DEATHDAY # '-NUMBER = 2/26/19/97 = 2 + 26 + 19 + 97 = 144

WAS '-BORN in the '-MONTH of ('-12); AND, '-DIED in the '-MONTH of ('-2) = 2(12's) = (12 x 12) = 144 = DEATH/DAY # '-NUMBER!!!~'

(144 + 61) = 205 = (25 + 0) = 25 = FRAGMENTED BIRTHDAY # '-NUMBER!!!~'

FRAGMENTED BIRTHDAY # '-NUMBER = 1 + 2 + 1 + 1 + 9 + 2 + 9 = 25

FRAGMENTED DEATHDAY # '-NUMBER = 2 + 2 + 6 + 1 + 9 + 9 + 7 = 36

(25 + 36) = 61 = BIRTHDAY # '-NUMBER!!!~'

BIRTHDAY # '-NUMBER = 61 = PART of DEATHDAY # '-NUMBER = 22(61)997

$(2 + 2 + 9 + 9 + 7) = 29 = $ RECIPROCAL $= 92 = $ "FLIP EVERY ('-9) OVER to a ('-6)"; "FLIP EVERY ('-2) OVER to a ('-7)" $= 67 = $ AGE of DEATH for ACTOR DAVID FITZGERALD DOYLE (CHARLIE'S ANGELS)!!!~'

BIRTHYEAR $= 29 = $ RECIPROCAL $= 92 = $ "FLIP EVERY ('-9) OVER to a ('-6)"; "FLIP EVERY ('-2) OVER to a ('-7)" $= 67 = $ AGE of DEATH for ACTOR DAVID FITZGERALD DOYLE (CHARLIE'S ANGELS)!!!~'

BIRTH/YEAR $= 19/29 = (1 \times 9)(2 - 9) = 97 = $ DEATH/YEAR!!!~'

BIRTH/YEAR $= 19/29 = (1 \times 9)(2 - 9) = 97 = $ "FLIP EVERY ('-9) OVER to a ('-6)" $= 67 = $ AGE of DEATH for ACTOR DAVID FITZGERALD DOYLE (CHARLIE'S ANGELS)!!!~'

BIRTH/YEAR $= 29 = $ RECIPROCAL $= 92 = $ "FLIP EVERY ('-2) OVER to a ('-7)" $= 97 = $ DEATH/YEAR!!!~'

DEATH/YEAR $= 19/97 = (1 + 9 + 9)(7) = (19)(7) = (97 \times 1) = 97 = $ "FLIP EVERY ('-9) OVER to a ('-6)" $= 67 = $ AGE of DEATH for ACTOR DAVID FITZGERALD DOYLE (CHARLIE'S ANGELS)!!!~'

DAY of DEATH $= 26 = $ RECIPROCAL $= 62 = $ "FLIP EVERY ('-2) OVER to a ('-7)" $= 67 = $ AGE of DEATH for ACTOR DAVID FITZGERALD DOYLE (CHARLIE'S ANGELS)!!!~'

DAY of DEATH $= 26 = $ "FLIP EVERY ('-6) OVER to a ('-9)" $= 29 = $ BIRTH/YEAR!!!~'

BIRTH/DAY $= 12/1 = (12 + 1) = 13$

DEATH/DAY $= 2/26 = (26 / 2) = 13$

(13 +13) = 26 = RECIPROCAL = 62 = "FLIP EVERY ('-2) OVER to a ('-7)" = 67 = AGE of DEATH for ACTOR DAVID FITZGERALD DOYLE (CHARLIE'S ANGELS)!!!~'

BIRTH/DAY = 12/1 = (21 + 1) = 22

FIRST PART of DEATH/DAY = (2/2)6

FROM BIRTH-TO-DEATH there are 87 DAYS = (8 x 7) = 56 = DEATHDAY # '-NUMBER = 144 = (14 x 4) = 56!!!~'

DEATH/YEAR = 19/97 = (97 (-) 19) = 78 = RECIPROCAL = 87

(365 (-) 87) = 278 = (2 – 8) (7) = 67 = AGE of DEATH for ACTOR DAVID FITZGERALD DOYLE (CHARLIE'S ANGELS)!!!~'

ACTOR CLAYTON MOORE (The LONE RANGER) died at the AGE of 85!!!~'

BIRTHDAY # '-NUMBER = 9/14/19/14 = 9 + 14 + 19 + 14 = 56

DEATHDAY # '-NUMBER = 12/28/19/99 = 12 + 28 + 19 + 99 = 158

DEATHDAY # '-NUMBER = 158 = RECIPROCAL = 851 = (85 x 1) = 85 = AGE of DEATH for ACTOR CLAYTON MOORE (The LONE RANGER)!!!~'

DEATHDAY # '-NUMBER in '-REVERSE = (99 (-) 19 (-) 28 (-) 12) = 40 = (8 X 5) = AGE of DEATH for ACTOR CLAYTON MOORE (The LONE RANGER)!!!~'

DEATH/DAY = 12/28 = RECIPROCAL = 82/21 = (82 + 2 + 1) = 85 = AGE of DEATH for ACTOR CLAYTON MOORE (The LONE RANGER)!!!~'

DAY of DEATH = 28 (x 2) = 56 = BIRTHDAY # `-NUMBER!!!~'

DAY of DEATH = 28 = "FLIP EVERY (`-2) OVER to a (`-7)" = 78 = (7 x 8) = 56 = BIRTHDAY # `-NUMBER!!!~'

BIRTH/YEAR = 19/14 = (1 – 9) (1 + 4) = 85 = AGE of DEATH for ACTOR CLAYTON MOORE (The LONE RANGER)!!!~'

BIRTH/DAY = 9/14 = BIRTH/YEAR = 1(914)!!!~'

BIRTH/MONTH = SEPTEMBER = 30!!!~'

(30 (-) 14) - (DAY of BIRTH) = 16 = RECIPROCAL = 61 = WAS 6' 1" in HEIGHT!!!~'

DEATH/DAY = 12/28 = (28 (-) 12) = 16 = RECIPROCAL = 61 = WAS 6' 1" in HEIGHT!!!~'

YEARS `-ACTIVE = (1934 to 1999) = 65 YEARS = RECIPROCAL = 56 = BIRTHDAY # `-NUMBER!!!~'

BIRTH/DAY = 9/14 = "FLIP EVERY (`-9) OVER to a (`-6)" = 6/14 = (6) (1 + 4) = 65!!!~'

ACTOR JAY SILVERHEELS (TONTO from the LONE RANGER) died at the AGE of 67!!!~'

BIRTHDAY # `-NUMBER = 5/26/19/12 = 5 + 26 + 19 + 12 = 62

DEATHDAY # `-NUMBER = 3/5/19/80 = 3 + 5 + 19 + 80 = 107

(107 (-) 62) = 45 = WAS `-MARRIED in 19(45) TO MARY DIROMA until 1980!!!~'

(107 + 62) = 169 = (16 x 9) = 144 = (44 + 1) = 45!!!~'

(107 + 62) = 169 = (69 x 1) = 69 = (6 x 9) = 54 = RECIPROCAL = 45!!!~'

`-ENDED HIS `-MARRIAGE to BOBBIE SMITH in 43; AND, was ACTIVE in HIS CAREER for 43 YEARS from 1937 to 1980!!!~'

ACTOR CLAYTON MOORE (The LONE RANGER) was `-ACTIVE from 19(34) TO 1999!!!~'

(`-34) = RECIPROCAL = (`-43)!!!~'

BIRTHDAY # `-NUMBER = 62 = "FLIP EVERY (`-2) OVER to a (`-7)" = 67 = AGE of DEATH for ACTOR JAY SILVERHEELS (TONTO from the LONE RANGER)!!!~'

DAY of BIRTH = 26 = RECIPROCAL = 62 = "FLIP EVERY (`-2) OVER to a (`-7)" = 67 = AGE of DEATH for ACTOR JAY SILVERHEELS (TONTO from the LONE RANGER)!!!~'

BIRTH/DAY = 5/26 = RECIPROCAL = 62/5 = (62 + 5) = 67 = AGE of DEATH for ACTOR JAY SILVERHEELS (TONTO from the LONE RANGER)!!!~'

DEATH/DAY = 3/5 = "FLIP EVERY (`-3) OVER to an (`-8)" = 85 = AGE of DEATH for ACTOR CLAYTON MOORE (The LONE RANGER)!!!~'

ACTOR CLAYTON MOORE (The LONE RANGER) `-DEATH/ YEAR = 19/99 = (99 (-) 19) = 80 = DEATH/YEAR for ACTOR JAY SILVERHEELS (TONTO from the LONE RANGER)!!!~'

DEATH/YEAR = 19/80 = (19 + 80) = 99 = DEATH/YEAR for ACTOR CLAYTON MOORE (The LONE RANGER)!!!~'

DEATH/YEAR = 19/80 = (80 (-) 19) = 61 = ACTOR CLAYTON MOORE (The LONE RANGER) was 6' 1" in HEIGHT!!!~'

DEATH/DAY # `-NUMBER in `-REVERSE = (80 (-) 19 (-) 5 (-) 3) = 53 = RECIPROCAL = 35 = DEATH/DAY!!!~'

WAS `-BORN in the `-MONTH of (`-5); AND, `-DIED in the `-MONTH of (`-3)!!!~'

FRAGMENTED BIRTHDAY # `-NUMBER = 5 + 2 + 6 + 1 + 9 + 1 + 2 = 26 = RECIPROCAL = 62 = "FLIP EVERY (`-2) OVER to a (`-7)" = 67 = AGE of DEATH for ACTOR JAY SILVERHEELS (TONTO from the LONE RANGER)!!!~'

FRAGMENTED DEATHDAY # `-NUMBER = 3 + 5 + 1 + 9 + 8 + 0 = 26 = RECIPROCAL = 62 = "FLIP EVERY (`-2) OVER to a (`-7)" = 67 = AGE of DEATH for ACTOR JAY SILVERHEELS (TONTO from the LONE RANGER)!!!~'

BIRTH/DAY # `-NUMBER = 62 = RECIPROCAL = 26 = (`-BOTH) FRAGMENTED BIRTHDAY # `-NUMBER & FRAGMENTED DEATH/DAY # `-NUMBER!!!~'

DEATH/MONTH = MARCH = 31!!!~'

(31 (-) 5) - (DAY of DEATH) = 26 = RECIPROCAL = 62 = "FLIP EVERY (`-2) OVER to a (`-7)" = 67 = AGE of DEATH for ACTOR JAY SILVERHEELS (TONTO from the LONE RANGER)!!!~'

FROM DAY of DEATH/MONTH = (31 (-) 5) - (DAY of DEATH) = 26 = DAY of BIRTH!!!~'

FROM BIRTH-TO-DEATH there are 82 DAYS!!!~'

(365 (-) 82) = 283 = (83 x 2) = 166 = (66 + 1) = 67 = AGE of DEATH for ACTOR JAY SILVERHEELS (TONTO from the LONE RANGER)!!!~'

(365 (-) 82) = 283 = RECIPROCAL = 382 = (38 x 2) = 76 = RECIPROCAL = 67 = AGE of DEATH for ACTOR JAY SILVERHEELS (TONTO from the LONE RANGER)!!!~'

(365 (-) 82) = 283 = (2 x 3) (8) = 68 = DIED within HIS 68th YEAR of EXISTENCE!!!~'

BIRTH/YEAR = 19/12 = (1 x 9) (1 x 2) = 92 = "FLIP EVERY ('-9) OVER to a ('-6)"; FLIP EVERY ('-2) OVER to a ('-7)" = 67 = AGE of DEATH for ACTOR JAY SILVERHEELS (TONTO from the LONE RANGER)!!!~'

DEATH/YEAR = 19/80 = (9 + 0) (1 - 8) = 97 = "FLIP EVERY ('-9) OVER to a ('-6)" = 67 = AGE of DEATH for ACTOR JAY SILVERHEELS (TONTO from the LONE RANGER)!!!~'

ACTOR GEORGE REEVES (SUPERMAN) died at the AGE of 45!!!~'

BIRTHDAY # '-NUMBER = 1/5/19/14 = 1 + 5 + 19 + 14 = 39

DEATHDAY # '-NUMBER = 6/16/19/59 = 6 + 16 + 19 + 59 = 100

(100 + 39) = 139 = (39 x 1) = 39

BIRTHDAY # `-NUMBER = 39 = WAS `-ACTIVE in HIS CAREER from 19(39) TO 1959!!!~'

WAS `-MARRIED to ELLANORA NEEDLES from 19(40) to 19(50) = 40/50 = (45 + 0 + 0) = 45 = AGE of DEATH for ACTOR GEORGE REEVES (SUPERMAN)!!!~'

(100 (-) 39) = 61!!!~' /|\ (`-162) = (62 (-) 1) = 61!!!~'

FIRST PART of `-DEATH/DAY = (6/1)6!!!~'

FROM BIRTH-TO-DEATH there are 162 DAYS = (1 + 2) (6) = 36 = "FLIP EVERY (`-6) OVER to a (`-9)" = 39 = BIRTHDAY # `-NUMBER!!!~'

(365 (-) 162) = 203 = (23 + 0) = 23 = -a PROPHETIC # `-NUMBER!!!~'

FRAGMENTED BIRTH/DAY # `-NUMBER = 1 + 5 + 1 + 9 + 1 + 4 = (`-21) = (3 X 7)!!!~'

FRAGMENTED DEATH/DAY # `-NUMBER = 6 + 1 + 6 + 1 + 9 + 5 + 9 = (`-37)!!!~'

(37 (-) 21) = (`-16) = RECIPROCAL = (`-61) = `-DEATH/DAY!!!~'

BIRTH/DAY = 1/5 = (1 + 5) = 6

WAS `-BORN in the MONTH of (`-1); AND, `-DIED in the `-MONTH of (`-6)!!!~'

SINGER/SONGWRITER ROY KELTON ORBISON died at the AGE of 52!!!~'

BIRTHDAY # `-NUMBER = 4/23/19/36 = 4 + 23 + 19 + 36 = 82

DEATHDAY # `-NUMBER = 12/6/19/88 = 12 + 6 + 19 + 88 = 125

BIRTHDAY # `-NUMBER = 82 = RECIPROCAL = 28 = 2(8's) = 88 = DEATH/YEAR!!!~'

DEATHDAY # `-NUMBER = 125 = RECIPROCAL = 521 = (52 x 1) = 52 = AGE of DEATH for SINGER/SONGWRITER ROY KELTON ORBISON!!!~'

DEATHDAY # `-NUMBER = 125 = RECIPROCAL = 521 = (52 + 1) = 53 = WAS `-ACTIVE from 19(53) to 19(88)!!!~'

BIRTH/DAY = 4/23 = (4) (2 + 3) = 45

DEATH/YEAR = 19/88 = (88 (-) 19) = 69 = (6 x 9) = 54 = RECIPROCAL = 45

BIRTH/DAY = 4/23 /|\ DEATH/DAY = 12/6

(4 + 23 + 12 + 6) = 45

BIRTH/DAY = 4/23 = (4 + 23) = 27

DEATH/DAY = 12/6 = (26 + 1) = 27

(27 + 27) = 54 = RECIPROCAL = 45

DEATH/MONTH = DECEMBER = 31 DAYS!!!~'

(31 (-) 6) - (DAY of DEATH) = 25 = RECIPROCAL = 52 = AGE of DEATH for SINGER/SONGWRITER ROY KELTON ORBISON!!!~'

FROM BIRTH-TO-DEATH there are 138 DAYS = RECIPROCAL = 831 = (83 (-) 1) = 82 = BIRTH/DAY # `-NUMBER!!!~'

(365 (-) 138) = 227 = (2 – 7) (2) = 52 = AGE of DEATH for SINGER/SONGWRITER ROY KELTON ORBISON!!!~'

FRAGMENTED BIRTHDAY # `-NUMBER = 4 + 2 + 3 + 1 + 9 + 3 + 6 = 28

FRAGMENTED DEATHDAY # `-NUMBER = 1 + 2 + 6 + 1 + 9 + 8 + 8 = 35

(28 + 35) = 63 = RECIPROCAL = 36 = `-BIRTH/YEAR!!!~'

WAS `-BORN in the `-MONTH of (`-4); AND, `-DIED in the `-MONTH of (`-12) = 4/12 = (4 + 1) (2) = 52 = AGE of DEATH for SINGER/SONGWRITER ROY KELTON ORBISON!!!~'

DEATH/DAY # `-NUMBER in `-REVERSE = (88 (-) 19 (-) 6 (-) 12) = (`-51); AND, `-DIED at the `-AGE of (`-52)!!!~'

SINGER/SONGWRITER THOMAS EARL PETTY died at the AGE of 66!!!~'

BIRTHDAY # `-NUMBER = 10/20/19/50 = 10 + 20 + 19 + 50 = 99

DEATHDAY # `-NUMBER = 10/2/20/17 = 10 + 2 + 20 + 17 = 49

BIRTHDAY # `-NUMBER = 99 = "FLIP EVERY (`-9) OVER to a (`-6)" = 66 = AGE of DEATH for SINGER/SONGWRITER THOMAS EARL PETTY!!!~'

DEATHDAY # `-NUMBER = 49 = (4 x 9) = 36 = 3(6's) = 666

BIRTH/DAY = 10/20

DEATH/DAY = 10/2 = JUST `-REMOVE the `-ZERO!!!~'

FRAGMENTED BIRTH/DAY # `-NUMBER = 1 + 0 + 2 + 0 + 1 + 9 + 5 + 0 = 18 = RECIPROCAL = 81 = (9 X 9) = BIRTH/DAY # `-NUMBER!!!~'

FRAGMENTED BIRTH/DAY # `-NUMBER = 1 + 0 + 2 + 0 + 1 + 9 + 5 + 0 = 18

FRAGMENTED DEATH/DAY # `-NUMBER = 1 + 0 + 2 + 2 + 0 + 1 + 7 = 13 = "FLIP EVERY (`-3) OVER to an (`-8)" = 18

`-AGE of `-DEATH = 66 = (6 x 6) = 36 = (3 x 6) = 18

BIRTHDAY # `-NUMBER = 10/20/19/50 = 10 + 20 + 19 + 50 = 99 = (9 + 9) = 18

FROM BIRTH-TO-DEATH there were 18 DAYS = (2 x 9) = 2(9's) = 99 = BIRTHDAY # `-NUMBER = "FLIP EVERY (`-9) OVER to a (`-6)" = 66 = AGE of DEATH for SINGER/SONGWRITER THOMAS EARL PETTY!!!~'

(365 (-) 18) = 347 = (3 + 4) (7) = 77 = (7 x 7) = 49 = DEATH/DAY # `-NUMBER!!!~'

BIRTH/YEAR = 19/50 = (19 + 50) = 69 = "FLIP EVERY (`-9) OVER to a (`-6)" = 66 = AGE of DEATH for SINGER/SONGWRITER THOMAS EARL PETTY!!!~'

WAS `-MARRIED to DANA YORK from 2001 to 2017 for 16 YEARS!!!~'

WAS `-MARRIED to JANE BENYO from 1974 to 19(96) for 22 YEARS!!!~'

DWAYNE W. ANDERSON

(`-22) = "FLIP EVERY (`-2) OVER to a (`-7)" = 77 = (7 x 7) = 49 = DEATH/DAY # `-NUMBER!!!~'

(22 (-) 16) = 6 (x 2) = 2(6's) = 66 = AGE of DEATH for SINGER/ SONGWRITER THOMAS EARL PETTY!!!~'

(22/16) = (2 / 2 + 1) (6) = 26 = 2(6's) = 66 = AGE of DEATH for SINGER/SONGWRITER THOMAS EARL PETTY!!!~'

`-AGE of `-DEATH = 66 = (6 / 6) = (`-1) = WAS `-BORN & `-DIED in the `-MONTH of (`-10) = JUST DROP the `-ZERO = (`-1)!!!~'

SINGER/SONGWRITER LITTLE RICHARD (RICHARD WAYNE PENNIMAN) died at the AGE of 87!!!~'

BIRTHDAY # `-NUMBER = 12/5/19/32 = 12 + 5 + 19 + 32 = 68

DEATHDAY # `=NUMBER = 5/9/20/20 = 5 + 9 + 20 + 20 = 54

BIRTH/YEAR = 19/32 = (1 x 9) (3 + 2) = 95 = RECIPROCAL = 59 = DEATH/DAY!!!~'

(68 + 54) = 122 = (22 + 1) = 23 = FRAGMENTED BIRTHDAY # `=NUMBER = RECIPROCAL = 32 = BIRTH/YEAR!!!~'

FRAGMENTED BIRTHDAY # `-NUMBER = 1 + 2 + 5 + 1 + 9 + 3 + 2 = 23 = RECIPROCAL = 32 = BIRTH/YEAR!!!~'

FRAGMENTED BIRTHDAY # `-NUMBER = 1 + 2 + 5 + 1 + 9 + 3 + 2 = 23 = RECIPROCAL = 32 = "FLIP EVERY (`-3) OVER to an (`-8)"; "FLIP EVERY (`-2) OVER to a (`-7)" = 87 = AGE of DEATH for SINGER/SONGWRITER LITTLE RICHARD (RICHARD WAYNE PENNIMAN)!!!~'

FRAGMENTED DEATHDAY # `-NUMBER = 5 + 9 + 2 + 0 + 2 + 0 = 18 = (6 X 3) = "FLIP EVERY (`-3) OVER to an (`-8)" = 68 = BIRTHDAY # `-NUMBER!!!~'

FROM BIRTH-TO-DEATH there are 155 DAYS = (55 (-) 1) = 54 = DEATH/DAY # `-NUMBER!!!~'

FROM BIRTH-TO-DEATH there are 155 DAYS = (55 + 1) = 56 = (8 X 7) = AGE of DEATH for SINGER/SONGWRITER LITTLE RICHARD (RICHARD WAYNE PENNIMAN)!!!~'

(365 (-) 155) = 210 = (21 + 0) = 21 = (3 X 7) = "FLIP EVERY (`-3) OVER to an (`-8)" = 87 = AGE of DEATH for SINGER/SONGWRITER LITTLE RICHARD (RICHARD WAYNE PENNIMAN)!!!~'

YEARS `-ACTIVE from 1947 to 2020 = 73 YEARS = RECIPROCAL = (`-37)!!!~'

DEATH/DAY = 5/9 = WAS `-MARRIED in 19(59) until 19(63) TO ERNESTINE CAMPBELL!!!~'

BIRTHDAY # `-NUMBER = 68 = "FLIP EVERY (`-8) OVER to a (`-3)" = (`-63)!!!~'

SINGER/SONGWRITER JOHNNY CASH (JOHN R. CASH) died at the AGE of 71!!!~'

DAY of DEATH = 12 = RECIPROCAL = 21 = "FLIP EVERY (`-2) OVER to a (`-7)" = 71 = AGE of DEATH for SINGER/SONGWRITER JOHNNY CASH (JOHN R. CASH)!!!~'

BIRTHDAY # `-NUMBER = 2/26/19/32 = 2 + 26 + 19 + 32 = 79

DWAYNE W. ANDERSON

DEATHDAY # `-NUMBER = 9/12/20/03 = 9 + 12 + 20 + 03 = 44

DEATH/DAY = 9/12 = (9) (1 x 2) = 92 = "FLIP EVERY (`-2) OVER to a (`-7)" = 97 = RECIPROCAL = 79 = BIRTHDAY # `-NUMBER!!!~'

(79 + 44) = 123 = (23 x 1) = (`-23) = DEATH/YEAR = (20 + 03) = 23 = RECIPROCAL = 32 = BIRTH/YEAR!!!~'

(79 (-) 44) = (`-35)!!!~'

WAS `-MARRIED to JUNE CARTER CASH from 1968 to 2003 for (`-35) YEARS!!!~'

WAS `-MARRIED to VIVIAN LIBERTO from 1954 to 1966 for (`-12) YEARS!!!~'

(`-12) = RECIPROCAL = 21 = "FLIP EVERY (`-2) OVER to a (`-7)" = 71 = AGE of DEATH for SINGER/SONGWRITER JOHNNY CASH (JOHN R. CASH)!!!~'

(35 (-) 12) = (`-23) = DEATH/YEAR = (20+03) = 23 = RECIPROCAL = 32 = BIRTH/YEAR!!!~'

DEATH/DAY = 9/12 = (9 + 12) = 21 = "FLIP EVERY (`-2) OVER to a (`-7)" = 71 = AGE of DEATH for SINGER/SONGWRITER JOHNNY CASH (JOHN R. CASH)!!!~'

FRAGMENTED BIRTHDAY # `-NUMBER = 2 + 2 + 6 + 1 + 9 + 3 + 2 = 25

FRAGMENTED DEATHDAY # `-NUMBER = 9 + 1 + 2 + 2 + 0 + 0 + 3 = 17 = RECIPROCAL = 71 = AGE of DEATH for SINGER/SONGWRITER JOHNNY CASH (JOHN R. CASH)!!!~'

(25 (-) 17) = 8 = (7 + 1) = 71 = AGE of DEATH for SINGER/ SONGWRITER JOHNNY CASH (JOHN R. CASH)!!!~'

(25 + 17) = 42 = "FLIP EVERY ('-2) OVER to a ('-7)" = 47

YEARS ACTIVE from 1954 to 2003 = 49

BIRTHDAY # '-NUMBER = 79 /|\ DEATHDAY # '-NUMBER = 44

(74) = RECIPROCAL = 47 /|\ (94) = RECIPROCAL = 49

BIRTHDAY # '-NUMBER = 79 = (7 + 9) = 16

DEATHDAY # '-NUMBER = 44 = (4 x 4) = 16

(16 + 16) = 32 = BIRTH/YEAR = RECIPROCAL = 23 = DEATH/ YEAR = (20 + 03) = ('-23)!!!~'

FROM BIRTH-TO-DEATH there are 198 DAYS = (1 – 8) (9) = 79 = BIRTHDAY # '-NUMBER!!!~'

(365 (-) 198) = 167 = RECIPROCAL = 761 = (76 x 1) = 76 = "FLIP EVERY ('-6) OVER to a ('-9)" = 79 = BIRTHDAY # '-NUMBER!!!~'

FORMER SENATE MAJORITY LEADER HARRY MASON REID JR. died at the AGE of 82!!!~'

DAY of DEATH = 28 = RECIPROCAL = 82 = AGE of DEATH for FORMER SENATE MAJORITY LEADER HARRY MASON REID JR.!!!~'

BIRTHDAY # '-NUMBER = 12/2/19/39 = 12 + 2 + 19 + 39 = 72

DEATHDAY # `-NUMBER = 12/28/20/21 = 12 + 28 + 20 + 21 = 81

(72 + 81) = 153 = "FLIP EVERY (`-3) to an (`-8)" = 158 = (58 + 1) = 59

WAS `-MARRIED to LANDRA GOULD from 19(59) to 2021 for 62 YEARS!!!~'

BIRTH/DAY = 12/2 = "FLIP EVERY (`-2) OVER to a (`-7)" = 17/2 = (1 + 7) (2) = 82 = AGE of DEATH for FORMER SENATE MAJORITY LEADER HARRY MASON REID JR.!!!~'

FRAGMENTED BIRTHDAY # `-NUMBER = 1 + 2 + 2 + 1 + 9 + 3 + 9 = 27 = RECIPROCAL = 72 = BIRTHDAY # `-NUMBER!!!~'

FRAGMENTED DEATHDAY # `-NUMBER = 1 + 2 + 2 + 8 + 2 + 0 + 2 + 1 = 18 = RECIPROCAL = 81 = DEATHDAY # `-NUMBER!!!~'

FROM BIRTH-TO-DEATH = 26 DAYS = RECIPROCAL = (`-62)!!!~'

WAS `-MARRIED to LANDRA GOULD from 19(59) to 2021 for (`-62) YEARS!!!~'

(365 (-) 26) = 339 = (3 x 3) (9) = 99 = (9 x 9) = 81 = DEATHDAY # `-NUMBER!!!~'

BIRTH/YEAR = 19(39) = (1 - 9) (3 + 9) = 8(12) = (82 x 1) = 82 = AGE of DEATH for FORMER SENATE MAJORITY LEADER HARRY MASON REID JR.!!!~'

FORMER U.S. SENATOR BOB DOLE (ROBERT JOSEPH DOLE) died at the AGE of 98!!!~'

BIRTHDAY # `-NUMBER = 7/22/19/23 = 7 + 22 + 19 + 23 = 71

DEATHDAY # `-NUMBER = 12/5/20/21 = 12 + 5 + 20 + 21 = 58

(71 + 58) = 129 = (29 x 1) = 29 = BIRTH/DAY = (7/22) = (7 + 22) = 29

WAS FIRST `-MARRIED in (`-1948) = (48 (-) 19) = (`-29)!!!~'

(71 (-) 58) = 13 = FRAGMENTED DEATHDAY # `-NUMBER!!!~'

DEATH/DAY = 12/5 = (12 + 5) = 17 = RECIPROCAL = 71 = BIRTHDAY # `-NUMBER!!!~'

(71) = (7 + 1) = (`-8) /|\

(58) = (5 + 8) = (`-13) = "FLIP EVERY (`-3) OVER to an (`-8)" = 18 = (1 + 8) = (`-9) /|\

(89) = RECIPROCAL = (`-98) = AGE of DEATH for FORMER U.S. SENATOR BOB DOLE (ROBERT JOSEPH DOLE)!!!~'

FRAGMENTED BIRTHDAY # `-NUMBER = 7 + 2 + 2 + 1 + 9 + 2 + 3 = 26

DEATH/DAY = 12/5 = (25 + 1) = 26 = FRAGMENTED BIRTHDAY # `-NUMBER!!!~'

FRAGMENTED DEATHDAY # `-NUMBER = 1 + 2 + 5 + 2 + 0 + 2 + 1 = 13 = (5 + 8) = 58 = DEATH/DAY # `-NUMBER!!!~'

FRAGMENTED BIRTHDAY # `-NUMBER = (26 / 2) = 13 = FRAGMENTED DEATHDAY # `-NUMBER!!!~'

(26 + 13) = 39 = (3 x 9) = 27 = RECIPROCAL = 72 = (9 X 8) = 98 = AGE of DEATH for FORMER U.S. SENATOR BOB DOLE (ROBERT JOSEPH DOLE)!!!~'

WAS `-MARRIED to ELIZABETH DOLE from 1975 to 2021 for (`-46) YEARS = (`-23 x (2)) = BIRTH/YEAR = (`-23)!!!~'

WAS `-MARRIED to PHYLLIS HOLDEN from 19(48) to 19(72) for (`-24) YEARS = RECIPROCAL = 42 = BIRTH/YEAR = (19 + 23) = (`-42)!!!~'

WAS `-MARRIED to PHYLLIS HOLDEN from 19(48) to 19(72) for (`-24) YEARS = DEATH/DAY = 12/5 = (25 (-) 1) = (`-24) x (2) = (`-48)!!!~'

ENDED MARRIAGE in (`-72) = BIRTH/DAY = (7/22)!!!~'

`-AGE of `-DEATH = (`-98) = (9 X 8) = (`-72)!!!~'

WAS `-BORN in the `-MONTH of (`-7); AND, `-DIED in the `-MONTH of (`-12) = (7/12) = (7 x 12) = 84 = RECIPROCAL = 48 = WAS `-FIRST `-MARRIED in (`-48)!!!~'

WAS `-BORN in the `-MONTH of (`-7); AND, `-DIED in the `-MONTH of (`-12) = (7/12) = (72 x 1) = (`-72) = (9 X 8) = 98 = AGE of DEATH for FORMER U.S. SENATOR BOB DOLE (ROBERT JOSEPH DOLE)!!!~'

FROM BIRTH-TO-DEATH there are 136 DAYS = (1 – 6) (3) = 53 = "FLIP EVERY (`-3) OVER to an (`-8)" = 58 = DEATH/DAY # `-NUMBER!!!~'

(365 (-) 136) = 229 = (22 (-) 9) = 13 = FRAGMENTED DEATH/ DAY # `-NUMBER!!!~'

AMERICAN FOOTBALL COACH & COMMENTATOR JOHN EARL MADDEN died at the AGE of 85!!!~'

DEATH/DAY = 12/28 = RECIPROCAL = 82/21 = (82 + 2 + 1) = 85 = AGE of DEATH for AMERICAN FOOTBALL COACH & COMMENTATOR JOHN EARL MADDEN!!!~'

BIRTHDAY # `-NUMBER = 4/10/19/36 = 4 + 10 + 19 + 36 = 69

DEATHDAY # `-NUMBER = 12/28/20/21 = 12 + 28 + 20 + 21 = 81

(81 (-) 69) = 12

DEATH/DAY # `-NUMBER = (12)/28/20/21 = (28 + 20 + 21) = 69 = BIRTH/DAY # `-NUMBER!!!~'

BIRTH/DAY = 4/10 = (4 x 10) = 40 = (8 X 5) = 85 = AGE of DEATH for AMERICAN FOOTBALL COACH & COMMENTATOR JOHN EARL MADDEN!!!~'

DEATH/DAY = 12/28 = (12 + 28) = 40 = (8 X 5) = 85 = AGE of DEATH for AMERICAN FOOTBALL COACH & COMMENTATOR JOHN EARL MADDEN!!!~'

FRAGMENTED BIRTHDAY # `-NUMBER = 4 + 1 + 0 + 1 + 9 + 3 + 6 = (`-24) = RECIPROCAL = (`-42)!!!~'

FRAGMENTED DEATHDAY # `-NUMBER = 1 + 2 + 2 + 8 + 2 + 0 + 2 + 1 = (`-18) = RECIPROCAL = (`-81) = DEATHDAY # `-NUMBER!!!~'

(24 + 18) = (`-42)

WAS `-MARRIED to VIRGINIA FIELDS from (1959) to 2021 for (`-62) YEARS!!!~'

WAS `-MARRIED in 19/59 = (59 (-) 19) = 40 = (8 X 5) = 85 = AGE of DEATH for AMERICAN FOOTBALL COACH & COMMENTATOR JOHN EARL MADDEN!!!~'

HIS CAREER END was in 19(58) = (`-58) = RECIPROCAL = (`-85) = AGE of DEATH for AMERICAN FOOTBALL COACH & COMMENTATOR JOHN EARL MADDEN!!!~'

FROM BIRTH-TO-DEATH there are 103 DAYS = (13 + 0) = 13 = (5 + 8) = 58 = RECIPROCAL = (`-85) = AGE of DEATH for AMERICAN FOOTBALL COACH & COMMENTATOR JOHN EARL MADDEN!!!~'

(365 (-) 103) = 262 = (2 – 6) (2) = 42 = RECIPROCAL = 24 = FRAGMENTED BIRTHDAY # `-NUMBER!!!~'

(`-26) = RECIPROCAL = (`-62)!!!~'

(365 (-) 103) = 262 = WAS `-MARRIED to VIRGINIA FIELDS from 1959 to 2021 for (`-**62**) YEARS!!!~'

AMERICAN SINGER, GUITARIST; and, PROFESSIONAL BASEBALL PLAYER (COUNTRY MUSIC LENGEND) CHARLEY FRANK PRIDE died at the AGE of 86!!!~'

BIRTHDAY # `-NUMBER 3/18/1934 = 3 + 18 + 19 + 34 = 74

DEATHDAY # `-NUMBER 12/12/20/20 = 12 + 12 + 20 + 20 = 64

(74 + 64) = 138 = "SWIPE 1" = (3/18) = BIRTH/DAY!!!~'

(74 (-) 64) = 10 = FRAGMENTED DEATHDAY # `-NUMBER!!!~'

FRAGMENTED BIRTHDAY # `-NUMBER = 3 + 1 + 8 + 1 + 9 + 3 + 4 = 29

FRAGMENTED DEATHDAY # `-NUMBER = 1 + 2 + 1 + 2 + 2 + 0 + 2 + 0 = 10

WAS `-MARRIED to ROZENE COHRAN from 1956 to 2020 for 64 YEARS = DEATH/DAY # `-NUMBER = (`-64)!!!~'

BIRTH/DAY = 3/18 = (3 + 18) = 21 = RECIPROCAL = 12 = DIED on 12/12!!!~'

FROM BIRTH-TO-DEATH there are 96 DAYS = (9 x 6) = 54 = (3 X 18) = BIRTH/DAY!!!~'

(365 (-) 96) = 269 = (69 x 2) = (`-138) = "SWIPE 1" = (3/18) = BIRTH/DAY!!!~'

(365 (-) 96) = 269 = (26 x 9) = 234 = (2 x 34) = (`-68) = RECIPROCAL = (`-86) = AGE of DEATH for AMERICAN SINGER, GUITARIST; and, PROFESSIONAL BASEBALL PLAYER (COUNTRY MUSIC LENGEND) CHARLEY FRANK PRIDE!!!~'

`-BORN in the `-MONTH of (`-3); AND, `-DIED in the `-MONTH of (`-12) = 3/12 = (3 x 12) = (`-36) = "FLIP EVERY (`-3) OVER to an (`-8)" = (`-86) = AGE of DEATH for AMERICAN SINGER, GUITARIST; and, PROFESSIONAL BASEBALL PLAYER (COUNTRY MUSIC LENGEND) CHARLEY FRANK PRIDE!!!~'

BIRTH/YEAR = 19/34 = 19 + 34 = (`-53)!!!~'

AMERICAN PROFESSIONAL BASEBALL PLAYER JEREMY DEAN GIAMBI died at the AGE of 47!!!~'

BIRTH/YEAR = 74 = RECIPROCAL = 47 = AGE of DEATH for AMERICAN PROFESSIONAL BASEBALL PLAYER JEREMY DEAN GIAMBI!!!~'

BIRTH/YEAR = 19/74 = (19 + 74) = 93 = "JUST `-ADD a `-ZERO" = 9/30 = BIRTH/DAY!!!~'

BIRTHDAY # `-NUMBER 9/30/19/74 = 9 + 30 + 19 + 74 = 132

DEATHDAY # `-NUMBER 2/9/20/22 = 2 + 9 + 20 + 22 = 53

BIRTH/DAY # `-NUMBER = 132 = (1 + 3) (2) = 42 = "FLIP EVERY (`-2) OVER to a (`-7)" = 47 = AGE of DEATH for AMERICAN PROFESSIONAL BASEBALL PLAYER JEREMY DEAN GIAMBI!!!~'

DEATH/YEAR = 20/22 = (20 + 22) = 42 = "FLIP EVERY (`-2) OVER to a (`-7)" = 47 = AGE of DEATH for AMERICAN PROFESSIONAL BASEBALL PLAYER JEREMY DEAN GIAMBI!!!~'

(132 + 53) = 185 = (18 + 5) = 23 = RECIPROCAL = 32 = BIRTHDAY # `-NUMBER = 132 = (32 x 1) = 32!!!~'

(132 + 53) = 185 = RECIPROCAL = 581 = (58 x 1) = 58 = "FLIP EVERY (`-8) OVER to a (`-3)" = 53 = DEATH/DAY # `-NUMBER!!!~'

(132 (-) 53) = 79 = "FLIP EVERY (`-7) OVER to a (`-2)" = 2/9 = DEATH/DAY!!!~'

FRAGMENTED BIRTHDAY # `-NUMBER = 9 + 3 + 0 + 1 + 9 + 7 + 4 = 33

FRAGMENTED DEATHDAY # `-NUMBER = 2 + 9 + 2 + 0 + 2 + 2 = 17

$(33 + 17) = 50$

HOME RUNS = 52

RUNS BATTED IN = 209 = $(29 + 0)$ = 2/9 = DEATH/DAY!!!~'

FROM BIRTH-TO-DEATH there are **132 DAYS = BIRTH/DAY # `-NUMBER = (`-132)!!!~'**

$(365 (-) 132) = 233 = (23 + 3) = 26$ = "FLIP EVERY (`-6) OVER to a (`-9)" = 2/9 = DEATH/DAY!!!~'

`-BORN in the `-MONTH of (`-9); AND, `-DIED in the `-MONTH of (`-2) = 9/2 = RECIPROCAL = 2/9 = DEATH/DAY!!!~'

MUSICAL ARTIST/ACTOR - MEAT LOAF - (MICHAEL LEE ADAY) was BORN in (47) = RECIPROCAL = (74) = AGE of DEATH!!!~' RAY FOSSE (AMERICAN BASEBALL PLAYER) was BORN in (47) & RECIPROCAL = (74) = AGE of DEATH!~' HIS `-BIRTHDAY # `-NUMBER = 4+4+19+47 = 74!~' This is a PATTERN in MY 11 BOOKS!!!~'

JEREMY DEAN GIAMBI BIRTH/YEAR = 74 = RECIPROCAL = 47 = AGE of DEATH for AMERICAN PROFESSIONAL BASEBALL PLAYER JEREMY DEAN GIAMBI!!!~' BIRTHDAY = 9+30+19+74 = 132 & DIED 132 DAYS from BIRTH-TO-DEATH!!!~' SAME for MEAT LOAF & RAY FOSSE BORN in 47 & DIED in 74 with FOSSE'S BIRTHDAY = 74!!!~'

AMERICAN ACTOR CHRISTOPHER SHANNON PENN died at the AGE of 40!!!~'

BIRTHDAY # `-NUMBER = 10/10/19/65 = 10 + 10 + 19 + 65 = 104

DEATHDAY # `-NUMBER = 1/24/20/06 = 1 + 24 + 20 + 06 = 51

(104 (-) 51) = 53 = "FLIP EVERY (`-3) OVER to an (`-8)" = 58 = (5 x 8) = 40 = AGE of DEATH for AMERICAN ACTOR CHRISTOPHER SHANNON PENN!!!~'

BIRTH/YEAR = 19/65 = (1 + 9) (6 x 5) = (10) (30) = (10 + 30) = 40 = AGE of DEATH for AMERICAN ACTOR CHRISTOPHER SHANNON PENN!!!~'

BIRTHDAY # `-NUMBER = 104 = RECIPROCAL = 401 = (40 x 1) = 40 = AGE of DEATH for AMERICAN ACTOR CHRISTOPHER SHANNON PENN!!!~'

BIRTHDAY # `-NUMBER = 104 = (10 x 4) = 40 = AGE of DEATH for AMERICAN ACTOR CHRISTOPHER SHANNON PENN!!!~'

BIRTH/YEAR = 65 = (6 x 5) = 30 = YEARS `-ACTIVE from 1976 to 2006!!!~'

FRAGMENTED BIRTHDAY # `-NUMBER = 1 + 0 + 1 + 0 + 1 + 9 + 6 + 5 = 23 = -a PROPHETIC # `-NUMBER!!!~'

DEATH/DAY = 1/24 = (1 – 24) = (`-23) = FRAGMENTED BIRTHDAY # `-NUMBER!!!~'

FRAGMENTED DEATHDAY # `-NUMBER = 1 + 2 + 4 + 2 + 0 + 0 + 6 = 15 = RECIPROCAL = 51 = DEATHDAY # `-NUMBER!!!~'

FRAGMENTED DEATHDAY # `-NUMBER = 15 = RECIPROCAL = 51 = JUST `-ADD a `-ZERO = HEIGHT was 5' 10' !!!~'

FROM BIRTH-TO-DEATH there are 106 DAYS = RECIPROCAL = 601 = (60 + 1) = 61 !!!~'

(365 (-) 106) = 259 = (2 + 59) = 61

(61 + 61) = 122 = (1 + 22) = 23 = FRAGMENTED BIRTHDAY # `-NUMBER!!!~'

WAS `-BORN in the `-MONTH of (`-10); AND, `-DIED in the `-MONTH of (`-1) = 10/1 = JUST `-ADD a `-ZERO = 10/10 = BIRTH/DAY!!!~'

BIRTH/DAY = 10/10 = (10 x 10) = 100

DEATH/DAY = 1/24 = (1 + 24) = 25

(100 / (`-DIVIDED by) 25 = 4 = JUST `-ADD a `-ZERO = 40 = AGE of DEATH for AMERICAN ACTOR CHRISTOPHER SHANNON PENN!!!~'

AUSTRALIAN ACTOR HEATH ANDREW LEDGER died at the AGE of 28!!!~'

BIRTHDAY # `-NUMBER = 4/4/19/79 = 4 + 4 + 19 + 79 = 106

BIRTHDAY # `-NUMBER = 106 = (10 + 6) = 16 = (1 x 6) = 6

BIRTH/DAY = 4/4 = (4 + 4) = 8 = DEATH/YEAR = (`-8)!!!~'

DEATHDAY # `-NUMBER = 1/22/20/08 = 1 + 22 + 20 + 08 = 51

DEATHDAY # `-NUMBER = 51 = (5 + 1) = 6

(106 + 51) = 157 = (15 (-) 7) = 8 = DEATH/YEAR!!!~'

DEATH/DAY = 1/22 = (1 + 22) = 23 = -a PROPHETIC # `-NUMBER!!!~'

DEATH/DAY = 1/22 = (1 + 22) = 23 = "FLIP EVERY (`-3) OVER to an (`-8)" = 28 = AGE of DEATH for AUSTRALIAN ACTOR HEATH ANDREW LEDGER!!!~'

DEATH/YEAR = 20/08 = (20 + 08) = 28 = AGE of DEATH for AUSTRALIAN ACTOR HEATH ANDREW LEDGER!!!~'

FRAGMENTED BIRTHDAY # `-NUMBER = 4 + 4 + 1 + 9 + 7 + 9 = 34

FRAGMENTED DEATHDAY # `-NUMBER = 1 + 2 + 2 + 2 + 0 + 0 + 8 = 15 = RECIPROCAL = 51 = DEATHDAY # `-NUMBER!!!~'

(34 + 15) = 49 = (4 x 9) = 36 = RECIPROCAL = 63 = (7 X 9) = BIRTH/YEAR!!!~'

(34 (-) 15) = 19 = "FLIP EVERY (`-9) OVER to a (`-6)" = 16 !!!~'

`-AGE of `-DEATH = 28 = (2 x 8) = 16 = BIRTH/DAY # `-NUMBER = 106 = (10 + 6) = 16 !!!~'

BIRTH/DAY = 4/4 = (4 x 4) = 16 = YEARS ACTIVE from 1992 to 2008 was 16 YEARS = RECIPROCAL = 61 = HEIGHT was = 6' 1" !!!~'

BIRTH/YEAR = 79 = (7 + 9) = 16 = RECIPROCAL = 61 = (SEE `-ABOVE)!!!~'

FROM BIRTH-TO-DEATH there are 72 DAYS = (9 x 8) = BIRTH/
YEAR = (19 + 79) !!!~'

(365 (-) 72) = 293 = (29 + 3) = 32 = RECIPROCAL = 23 = "FLIP
EVERY ('-3) OVER to an ('-8)" = 28 = AGE of DEATH for
AUSTRALIAN ACTOR HEATH ANDREW LEDGER!!!~'

WAS '-BORN in the '-MONTH of ('-4); AND, '-DIED in the
'-MONTH of ('-1) = 4/1 = RECIPROCAL = 14 (x TIMES) ('-2) = 28
= AGE of DEATH for AUSTRALIAN ACTOR HEATH ANDREW
LEDGER!!!~'

BIRTH/YEAR = 19/79 = (1 – 9) (7 – 9) = 82 = RECIPROCAL = 28
= AGE of DEATH for AUSTRALIAN ACTOR HEATH ANDREW
LEDGER!!!~'

AMERICAN SINGER/ACTOR/COMEDIAN DEAN MARTIN
died at the AGE of 78!!!~'

BIRTHDAY # '-NUMBER = 6/7/19/17 = 6 + 7 + 19 + 17 = 49

DEATHDAY # '-NUMBER = 12/25/19/95 = 12 + 25 + 19 + 95 = 151

DEATH/DAY # '-NUMBER in '-REVERSE = (95 (-) 19 (-) 25 (-)
12) = 39 (X TIMES) ('-2) = 78 = AGE of DEATH for AMERICAN
SINGER/ACTOR/COMEDIAN DEAN MARTIN!!!~'

(151 (-) 49) = 102 = RECIPROCAL = 201 = DAYS from
BIRTH-TO-DEATH!!!~'

DEATH/DAY = 12/25 = (12 + 25) = 37 = RECIPROCAL = 73
= "FLIP EVERY ('-3) OVER to an ('-8)" = 78 = AGE of DEATH

for AMERICAN SINGER/ACTOR/COMEDIAN DEAN MARTIN!!!~'

BIRTH/DAY = 6/7 = (6 + 7) = 13 = "SEE BELOW"!!!~'

DEATH/DAY = 12/25 = (12 − 25) = 13 = RECIPROCAL = 31 = FRAGMENTED BIRTH/DAY # `-NUMBER!!!~'

FRAGMENTED BIRTHDAY # `-NUMBER = 6 + 7 + 1 + 9 + 1 + 7 = 31

FRAGMENTED DEATHDAY # `-NUMBER = 1 + 2 + 2 + 5 + 1 + 9 + 9 + 5 = 34

(31 + 34) = 65 = RECIPROCAL = 56!!!~'

`-AGE of `-DEATH = 78 = (7 x 8) = 56!!!~'

YEARS `-ACTIVE from 1932 TO 1988 = 56 YEARS!!!~'

DEATH/YEAR = 95 = RECIPROCAL = 59 = "FLIP EVERY (`-9) OVER to a (`-6)" = 56!!!~'

BIRTH/MONTH = JUNE = 30 DAYS!!!~'

(30 (-) 7) - (DAY of -BIRTH) = 23 = "FLIP EVERY (`-2) OVER to a (`-7)"; "FLIP EVERY (`-3) OVER to an (`-8)" = 78 = AGE of DEATH for AMERICAN SINGER/ACTOR/COMEDIAN DEAN MARTIN!!!~'

FROM BIRTH-TO-DEATH there are 201 DAYS = "SEE ABOVE"!!!~'

(365 (-) 201) = 164 = (64 + 1) = 65 = RECIPROCAL = "SEE ABOVE" = 56 = (7 X 8) = AGE of DEATH for AMERICAN SINGER/ACTOR/ COMEDIAN DEAN MARTIN!!!~'

BIRTH/YEAR = 19/17 = (1 – 9) (1 x 7) = 87 = RECIPROCAL = 78 = AGE of DEATH for AMERICAN SINGER/ACTOR/COMEDIAN DEAN MARTIN!!!~'

DEATH/YEAR = 19/95 = (95 (-) 19) = 76 = RECIPROCAL = 6/7 = BIRTH/DAY!!!~'

AMERICAN SINGER/ACTOR/COMEDIAN/DANCER SAMUEL GEORGE DAVIS JR. died at the AGE of 64!!!~'

BIRTH/DAY # `-NUMBER = 64 = AGE of DEATH for AMERICAN SINGER/ACTOR/COMEDIAN/DANCER SAMUEL GEORGE DAVIS JR.!!!~'

BIRTHDAY # `-NUMBER = 12/8/19/25 = 12 + 8 + 19 + 25 = 64

DEATHDAY # `-NUMBER = 5/16/19/90 = 5 + 16 + 19 + 90 = 130

DEATHDAY # `-NUMBER = 130 = (13 + 0) = 13 = RECIPROCAL = 31 = FRAGMENTED DEATH/DAY # `-NUMBER!!!~'

(64 + 130) = 194 = (1 + 94) = 95 = DEATH/YEAR for AMERICAN SINGER/ACTOR/COMEDIAN DEAN MARTIN!!!~'

FRAGMENTED BIRTHDAY # `-NUMBER = 1 + 2 + 8 + 1 + 9 + 2 + 5 = 28

FRAGMENTED DEATHDAY # `-NUMBER = 5 + 1 + 6 + 1 + 9 + 9 + 0 = 31

(28 + 31) = 59 = RECIPROCAL = 95 = DEATH/YEAR for AMERICAN SINGER/ACTOR/COMEDIAN DEAN MARTIN!!!~'

FROM BIRTH-TO-DEATH there are 159 DAYS = RECIPROCAL
= 951 = (95 x 1) = 95 = "SEE ABOVE"!!!~'

FROM BIRTH-TO-DEATH there are 159 DAYS = RECIPROCAL
= 951 = (95 + 1) = 96 = BIRTH/DAY = (12 x 8)!!!~'

(365 (-) 159) = 206 = RECIPROCAL = 602 = (60 + 2) = 62 = YEARS
`-ACTIVE from 1928 TO 1990 = 62 YEARS!!!~'

DEATH/DAY = 5/16 = (5 – 1) (6) = 46 = RECIPROCAL = 64 = AGE
of DEATH for AMERICAN SINGER/ACTOR/COMEDIAN/
DANCER SAMUEL GEORGE DAVIS JR.!!!~'

BIRTH/YEAR = 19/25 = (9) (5 – 2 + 1) = 94 = "FLIP EVERY (`-9)
OVER to a (`-6)" = 64 = AGE of DEATH for AMERICAN SINGER/
ACTOR/COMEDIAN/DANCER SAMUEL GEORGE DAVIS JR.!!!~'

ENGLISH-BORN AMERICAN ACTOR PETER SYDNEY
ERNEST LAWFORD died at the AGE of 61!!!~'

BIRTH/DAY = 9/7 = (9 + 7) = 16 = RECIPROCAL = 61 = AGE
of DEATH for ENGLISH-BORN AMERICAN ACTOR PETER
SYDNEY ERNEST LAWFORD!!!~'

BIRTHDAY # `-NUMBER = 9/7/19/23 = 9 + 7 + 19 + 23 = 58

(`-58) = (5 + 8) = 13 = RECIPROCAL = 31 = (`-SEE `-BELOW")!!!~'

DEATHDAY # `-NUMBER = 12/24/19/84 = 12 + 24 + 19 + 84 = 139

DEATH/DAY # `-NUMBER = 139 = (13 x 9) = 117 = (1) (1 – 7) =
16 = RECIPROCAL = 61 = AGE of DEATH for ENGLISH-BORN
AMERICAN ACTOR PETER SYDNEY ERNEST LAWFORD!!!~'

('-139) = (1 x 39) = 39 = "FLIP EVERY ('-9) OVER to a ('-6)" = 36

(139 (-) 58) = 81 = "FLIP EVERY ('-8) OVER to a ('-3)" = 31 = (BOTH) FRAGMENTED BIRTH/DAY & DEATH/DAY # '-NUMBERS!!!~'

BIRTH/DAY = 9/7 = (9 x 7) = 63 = RECIPROCAL = 36

DEATH/DAY = 12/24 = (12 + 24) = 36

FRAGMENTED BIRTHDAY # '-NUMBER = 9 + 7 + 1 + 9 + 2 + 3 = 31

FRAGMENTED DEATHDAY # '-NUMBER = 1 + 2 + 2 + 4 + 1 + 9 + 8 + 4 = 31

FRAGMENTED BIRTH/DAY # '-NUMBER = 31 = FRAGMENTED DEATH/DAY # '-NUMBER!!!~'

(31 / 31) = (3 + 3) (1 x 1) = 61 = AGE of DEATH for ENGLISH-BORN AMERICAN ACTOR PETER SYDNEY ERNEST LAWFORD!!!~'

HEIGHT = 5' 11" = (5 + 1) (1) = 61 = AGE of DEATH for ENGLISH-BORN AMERICAN ACTOR PETER SYDNEY ERNEST LAWFORD!!!~'

DEATH/DAY = 12/24 = HALF RECIPROCAL = 12/42 = (12 + 42) = 54 = YEARS '-ACTIVE from 1930 TO 1984 = 54 YEARS!!!~'

BIRTH/YEAR = 19/23 = (19 + 23) = 42 = RECIPROCAL = 24 = DAY OF DEATH = 24th!!!~'

WAS '-BORN in the '-MONTH of ('-9); AND, '-DIED in the '-MONTH of ('-12) = 9/12 = (9 x 12) = 108 !!!~'

FROM BIRTH-TO-DEATH there are 108 DAYS = RECIPROCAL = 801 = (80 + 1) = 81 = "SEE ABOVE"!!!~'

(365 (-) 108) = 257 = (25 + 7) = 32 = RECIPROCAL = 23 = BIRTH/YEAR!!!~'

DEATH/YEAR = 84 = (8 x 4) = 32 = RECIPROCAL = 23 = BIRTH/YEAR!!!~'

DEATH/YEAR = 19/84 = (19 + 84) = 103 = (10 + 3) = 13 = (5 + 8) = BIRTH/DAY # `-NUMBER = ("SEE `-ABOVE")!!!~'

WAS `-BORN in the `-MONTH of (`-9); AND, `-DIED in the `-MONTH of (`-12) = 9/12 = (9) (1 x 2) = 92 = "FLIP EVERY (`-2) OVER to a (`-7)" = 9/7 = BIRTH/DAY!!!~'

AMERICAN TRACK & FIELD ATHLETE JAMES CLEVELAND (JESSE) OWENS died at the AGE of 66!!!~'

BIRTHDAY # `-NUMBER = 9/12/19/13 = 9 + 12 + 19 + 13 = 53

BIRTHDAY # `-NUMBER = 53 = RECIPROCAL = 35 = WAS `-MARRIED in (`-35)!!!~'

DEATHDAY # `-NUMBER = 3/31/19/80 = 3 + 31 + 19 + 80 = 133

BIRTH/YEAR = 19/13 = (19 + 13) = 32

DEATH/DAY # `-NUMBER = 133 = (1 – 33) = 32 = BIRTH/YEAR!!!~'

(32 + 133) = 165 = DAYS from BIRTH-TO-DEATH = (1 + 65) = 66 = AGE of DEATH for AMERICAN TRACK & FIELD ATHLETE JAMES CLEVELAND (JESSE) OWENS!!!~'

(133 (-) 53) = 80 = DEATH/YEAR!!!~'

BIRTH/DAY = 9/12 = (9 x 12) = 108 = RECIPROCAL = 801 = (80 x 1) = 80 = DEATH/YEAR!!!~'

BIRTH/DAY = 9/12 = (91 + 2) = 93

DEATH/DAY = 3/31 = (3 x 31) = 93

WAS `-BORN in the `-MONTH of (`-9); AND, `-DIED in the `-MONTH of (`-3) = 9/3 !!!~'

FRAGMENTED BIRTHDAY # `-NUMBER = 9 + 1 + 2 + 1 + 9 + 1 + 3 = 26

FRAGMENTED BIRTHDAY # `-NUMBER = 26 = 2(6's) = 66 = AGE of DEATH for AMERICAN TRACK & FIELD ATHLETE JAMES CLEVELAND (JESSE) OWENS!!!~'

FRAGMENTED DEATHDAY # `-NUMBER = 3 + 3 + 1 + 1 + 9 + 8 + 0 = 25

(26 + 25) = 51 = RECIPROCAL = 15

(51 + 15) = 66 = AGE of DEATH for AMERICAN TRACK & FIELD ATHLETE JAMES CLEVELAND (JESSE) OWENS!!!~'

FROM BIRTH-TO-DEATH there are 165 DAYS = (65 + 1) = 66 = AGE of DEATH for AMERICAN TRACK & FIELD ATHLETE JAMES CLEVELAND (JESSE) OWENS!!!~'

(365 (-) 165) = 200 = (20 + 0) = 20 = (4 X 5) = MARRIED to MINNIE RUTH SOLOMON from 1935 TO 1980 for 45 YEARS!!!~'

BIRTH MONTH = SEPTEMBER = 30 DAYS!!!~'

DWAYNE W. ANDERSON

(30 (-) 12) – (DAY of BIRTH) = 18 = RECIPROCAL = 81 = (9 x 9) = 99 = "FLIP EVERY (`-9) OVER to a (`-6)" = 66 = AGE of DEATH for AMERICAN TRACK & FIELD ATHLETE JAMES CLEVELAND (JESSE) OWENS!!!~'

DEATHDAY = 19/80 = (19 + 80) = 99 = "FLIP EVERY (`-9) OVER to a (`-6)" = 66 = AGE of DEATH for AMERICAN TRACK & FIELD ATHLETE JAMES CLEVELAND (JESSE) OWENS!!!~'

AMERICAN PROFESSIONAL BASKETBALL PLAYER WILTON NORMAN CHAMBERLAIN died at the AGE of 63!!!~'

BIRTH/YEAR = 36 = RECIPROCAL = 63 = AGE of DEATH for AMERICAN PROFESSIONAL BASKETBALL PLAYER WILTON NORMAN CHAMBERLAIN!!!~'

BIRTHDAY # `-NUMBER = 8/21/19/36 = 8 + 21 + 19 + 36 = 84

BIRTHDAY # `-NUMBER = 84 = (8 x 4) = 32 = FRAGMENTED DEATH/DAY # `-NUMBER!!!~'

DEATHDAY # `-NUMBER = 10/12/19/99 = 10 + 12 + 19 + 99 = 140

(140 (-) 84) = 56 = (5 x 6) = 30 = FRAGMENTED BIRTHDAY # `-NUMBER!!!~'

(84 + 140) = 224 = (22 (-) 4) = 18 = (6 X 3) = AGE of DEATH for AMERICAN PROFESSIONAL BASKETBALL PLAYER WILTON NORMAN CHAMBERLAIN!!!~'

BIRTH/DAY = 8/21 = (8 + 21) = 29 = 2(9's) = 99 = DEATH/YEAR!!!~'

DAY of '-BIRTH = 21 = RECIPROCAL = 12 = DAY of '-DEATH!!!~'

FRAGMENTED BIRTHDAY # '-NUMBER = 8 + 2 + 1 + 1 + 9 + 3 + 6 = 30

FRAGMENTED DEATHDAY # '-NUMBER = 1 + 0 + 1 + 2 + 1 + 9 + 9 + 9 = 32

(30 + 32) = 62 = ONE '-YEAR '-AWAY from AGE of '-DEATH = 63 !!!~'

FRAGMENTED DEATHDAY # '-NUMBER = 32 = -a PROPHETIC # '-NUMBER!!!~'

BIRTH/YEAR = 19/36 = (36 (-) 19) = 17 = RECIPROCAL = 71 = HEIGHT = 7' 1" !!!~'

FROM BIRTH-TO-DEATH there are 52 DAYS = (5 x 2) = 10 = MONTH of '-DEATH!!!~'

(365 (-) 52) = 313 = (3 x 13) = 39 = RECIPROCAL = 93 = "FLIP EVERY ('-9) OVER to a ('-6)" = 63 = AGE of DEATH for AMERICAN PROFESSIONAL BASKETBALL PLAYER WILTON NORMAN CHAMBERLAIN!!!~'

(365 (-) 52) = 313 = (31 x 3) = 93 = "FLIP EVERY ('-9) OVER to a ('-6)" = 63 = AGE of DEATH for AMERICAN PROFESSIONAL BASKETBALL PLAYER WILTON NORMAN CHAMBERLAIN!!!~'

DEATH/YEAR = 19/99 = (99 (-) 19) = 80 = (8 x 10)!!!~'

WAS '-BORN in the '-MONTH of ('-8); AND, '-DIED in the '-MONTH of ('-10) = 8/10 = (8 + 10) = 18 = DEATH/YEAR = (19 + 99) = 118 = RECIPROCAL = 811 = (81 x 1) = 81 !!!~'

AGE of `-DEATH = (`-63) = (6 x 3) = 18 = RECIPROCAL = 81 !!!~'

DEATH/YEAR = 99 = (9 x 9) = 81

DEATH/YEAR = 99 = "FLIP EVERY (`-9) OVER to a (`-6)" = 66 = (6 x 6) = 36 = BIRTH/YEAR = RECIPROCAL = 63 = AGE of DEATH for AMERICAN PROFESSIONAL BASKETBALL PLAYER WILTON NORMAN CHAMBERLAIN!!!~'

BIRTH/MONTH = AUGUST = 31 DAYS!!!~'

(31 (-) 21 – (DAY of BIRTH) = 10 = MONTH of `-DEATH!!!~'

AMERICAN BASKETBALL PLAYER NATHANIEL THURMOND (GOLDEN STATE WARRIORS) died at the -AGE of 74!!!~'

BIRTHDAY # `-NUMBER = 7/25/19/41 = 7 + 25 + 19 + 41 = 92

DEATHDAY # `-NUMBER = 7/16/20/16 = 7 + 16 + 20 + 16 = 59

BIRTH/DAY = 7/25 = HALF RECIPROCAL = 7/52 = (7 + 52) = 59 = DEATHDAY # `-NUMBER!!!~'

(92 + 59) = 151 = (1 + 5) (1) = 61 = HEIGHT = 6' 11"

FRAGMENTED BIRTHDAY # `-NUMBER = 7 + 2 + 5 + 1 + 9 + 4 + 1 = 29

FRAGMENTED BIRTHDAY # `-NUMBER = 29 = RECIPROCAL = 92 = BIRTHDAY # `-NUMBER!!!~'

FRAGMENTED DEATHDAY # `-NUMBER = 7 + 1 + 6 + 2 + 0 + 1 + 6 = 23

(29 + 23) = 52 = RECIPROCAL = 25 = "FLIP EVERY (`-2) OVER to a (`-7)" = 75 = DIED 9 DAYS AWAY from TURNING (`-75)!!!~'

FRAGMENTED DEATHDAY # `-NUMBER = 23 = MARRIED for 23 YEARS!!!~'

BIRTH/DAY = 7/25 = (7 + 25) = 32 = RECIPROCAL = 23 !!!~'

DEATH/DAY = 7/16 = (7 + 16) = 23 !!!~'

WAS `-MARRIED to MARCI THURMOND from 19(93) TO 2016 for 23 YEARS!!!~'

(`-23) = -a PROPHETIC # `-NUMBER!!!~'

BIRTHDAY # `-NUMBER = 92 / (DIVIDED `-by) (4) = (`-23)!!!~'

(92/4) = (9 – 2) (4) = 74 = AGE of DEATH for AMERICAN BASKETBALL PLAYER NATHANIEL THURMOND (GOLDEN STATE WARRIORS)!!!~'

`-AGE of `-DEATH = 74 = (7 x 4) = 28 = "FLIP EVERY (`-8) OVER to a (`-3) = (`-23)!!!~'

FROM BIRTH-TO-DEATH there are 9 DAYS !!!~'

(365 (-) 9) = 356 = (35 + 6) = 41 = BIRTH/YEAR!!!~'

(365 (-) 9) = 356 = (3 + 56) = 59 = DEATHDAY # `-NUMBER!!!~'

WAS `-BORN in the `-MONTH of (`-7); AND, `-DIED in the `-MONTH of (`-7) = 7/7 = (7 + 7) = 14 = RECIPROCAL = 41 = BIRTH/YEAR!!!~'

BIRTH/DAY = 7/25 = 75 (2) = DIED 9 DAYS AWAY from TURNING (`-75)!!!~'

DEATH/DAY = 7/16 = (7) (1 – 6) = 75 = DIED 9 DAYS AWAY from TURNING (`-75)!!!~'

BIRTH/YEAR = 19/41 = (9 – 1 – 1) (4) = 74 = AGE of DEATH for AMERICAN BASKETBALL PLAYER NATHANIEL THURMOND (GOLDEN STATE WARRIORS)!!!~'

AMERICAN ACTOR PAUL WILLIAM WALKER IV died at the AGE of 40!!!~'

BIRTHDAY # `-NUMBER in `-REVERSE = (73 (-) 19 (-) 12 (-) 9) = (`-33) = DEATH/YEAR = (20 + 13) = (`-33)!!!~'

BIRTHDAY # `-NUMBER = 9/12/19/73 = 9 + 12 + 19 + 73 = 113

BIRTHDAY # `-NUMBER = 113 = (13 x 1) = 13 = DEATH/YEAR!!!~'

BIRTHDAY # `-NUMBER = 113 = (13 x 1) = 13 = DEATH/YEAR = 13 = (8 + 5) = (8 x 5) = 40 = AGE of DEATH for AMERICAN ACTOR PAUL WILLIAM WALKER IV!!!~'

BIRTHDAY # `-NUMBER = 113 = (11 x 3) = 33 = DEATH/YEAR = (20 + 13) = 33!!!~'

DEATHDAY # `-NUMBER = 11/30/20/13 = 11 + 30 + 20 + 13 = 74

(113 + 74) = 187 = RECIPROCAL = 781 = (7) (8 + 1) = 79 = DAYS from BIRTH-TO-DEATH!!!~'

DEATHDAY # `-NUMBER = 74 = (7 x 4) = 28

BIRTH/DAY = 9/12 = RECIPROCAL = 219 = (2) (1 - 9) = 28

BIRTH/DAY = 9/12 = (9 + 12) = 21

DEATH/DAY = 11/30 = (30 (-) 11) = 19

(21 + 19) = 40 = AGE of DEATH for AMERICAN ACTOR PAUL WILLIAM WALKER IV!!!~'

(113 (-) 74) = 39 = "FLIP EVERY (`-9) OVER to a (`-6)" = 36 = RECIPROCAL = 63 = (7 X 9) = DAYS from BIRTH-TO-DEATH!!!~'

(113 (-) 74) = 39 = RECIPROCAL = 93 = BIRTH/DAY = 9/12 = (91 + 2) = 93

BIRTH/DAY = 9/12 = HALF RECIPROCAL = 9/21 = (9 + 21) = 30 = DAY of DEATH!!!~'

`-AGE of `-DEATH = 40 = 4 x 10 = (4 + 10) = 14 = RECIPROCAL = 41 !!!~'

DEATH/DAY = 11/30 = (11 + 30) = 41 !!!~'

FRAGMENTED BIRTHDAY # `-NUMBER = 9 + 1 + 2 + 1 + 9 + 7 + 3 = 32 = -a PROPHETIC # `-NUMBER!!!~'

FRAGMENTED DEATHDAY # `-NUMBER = 1 + 1 + 3 + 0 + 2 + 0 + 1 + 3 = 11

(32 + 11) = 43 = (4 x 3) = 12 = DAY of `-BIRTH!!!~'

(32 (-) 11) = 21 = (7 X 3) = BIRTH/YEAR!!!~'

BIRTH/DAY = 9/12 = RECIPROCAL = 21/9 = "FLIP EVERY (`-2) OVER to a (`-7)" = 71/9 = (71 + 9) = 80 (DIVIDED by) (`-2) = 40 = AGE of DEATH for AMERICAN ACTOR PAUL WILLIAM WALKER IV!!!~'

BIRTH/DAY = 9/12 = RECIPROCAL = 21/9 = "FLIP EVERY (`-2) OVER to a (`-7)" = 71/9 = (79 x 1) = 79 = DAYS from BIRTH-TO-DEATH!!!~'

FROM BIRTH-TO-DEATH there are 79 DAYS = "FLIP EVERY (`-7) OVER to a (`-2)" = 29 = YEARS `-ACTIVE from 1984 TO 2013 for 29 YEARS!!!~'

WAS `-BORN in the `-MONTH of (`-9); AND, `-DIED in the `-MONTH of (`-11) = 9/11 = (9) (1 + 1) = 92 = RECIPROCAL = 29 !!!~'

BIRTH/YEAR = 19/73 = (19 + 73) = 92 = RECIPROCAL = 29

WAS `-BORN in the `-MONTH of (`-9); AND, `-DIED in the `-MONTH of (`-11) = 9/11 = (9 + 11) = 20 (X TIMES) (`-2) = 40 = AGE of DEATH for AMERICAN ACTOR PAUL WILLIAM WALKER IV!!!~'

(365 (-) 79) = 286 = (28 + 6) = 34 = RECIPROCAL = 43 = (4 x 3) = 12 = DAY of `-BIRTH!!!~'

BIRTH/MONTH = SEPTEMBER = 30 DAYS!!!~'

(30 (-) 12) – (DAY of BIRTH) = 18 = (6 X 3) = 63 = (7 X 9) = 79 = DAYS from BIRTH-TO-DEATH!!!~'

BIRTH/YEAR = 19/73 = (1 + 9) (7 – 3) = (10) (4) = (10 x 4) = 40 = AGE of DEATH for AMERICAN ACTOR PAUL WILLIAM WALKER IV!!!~'

SWEDISH ACTRESS INGRID BERGMAN died at the AGE of 67!!!~'

BIRTHDAY # '-NUMBER = 8/29/1915 = 8 + 29 + 19 + 15 = 71

DEATHDAY # '-NUMBER = 8/29/19/82 = 8 + 29 + 19 + 82 = 138

DEATH/DAY # -NUMBER = 138 = (13 + 8) = 21 = "FLIP EVERY ('-2) OVER to a ('-7)" = 71 = BIRTHDAY # '-NUMBER!!!~'

(71 + 138) = 209 = (29 + 0) = 29 = DAY of BIRTH & DAY of DEATH!!!~'

(138 (-) 71) = 67 = AGE of DEATH for SWEDISH ACTRESS INGRID BERGMAN!!!~'

BIRTH/DAY /|\ DEATH/DAY = 8/29 = SWIPE 2 to the LEFT = 9/82 = JUST '-ADD a ('-1) AND = DEATH/YEAR = 1982!!!~'

(8/29) = 8 + 29 = 37 = DEATH/DAY # '-NUMBER = 138 = (1 – 38) = 37

(8/29) = 8 + 29 = 37 = (3 x 7) = 21 = "FLIP EVERY ('-2) OVER to a ('-7)" = 71 = BIRTHDAY # '-NUMBER!!!~'

(8/29) = (29 (-) 8) = 21 = "FLIP EVERY ('-2) OVER to a ('-7)" = 71 = BIRTHDAY # '-NUMBER!!!~'

(8/29) = (8x29) = 232 = Reciprocal-Sequencing-Numerology-RSN!!!~'

YEARS '-ACTIVE started in 1932!!!~'

(32 (-) 19) = 13 = (6 + 7) = 67 = AGE of DEATH for SWEDISH ACTRESS INGRID BERGMAN!!!~'

BIRTH/DAY = 8/29 = DEATH/DAY = 8/29

BIRTH/DAY = 8/29 = (8 + 29) = 37

DEATH/DAY = 8/29 = (8 + 29) = 37

(37 + 37) = 74 = FRAG BIRTH/DEATH DAYS `-ADDED `-UP `-TOGETHER!!!~'

FRAGMENTED BIRTHDAY # `-NUMBER = 8 + 2 + 9 + 1 + 9 + 1 + 5 = 35

FRAGMENTED DEATHDAY # `-NUMBER = 8 + 2 + 9 + 1 + 9 + 8 + 2 = 39

(35 + 39) = 74

FROM BIRTH-TO-DEATH there are 0 DAYS!!!~'

(365 (-) 0) = 365 = (65 + 3) = 68 = "FLIP EVERY (`-8) OVER to a (`-3)" = 63 = DEATH/YEAR = (19 – 82) = 63!!!~'

(365 (-) 0) = 365 = (3 x 65) = 195 = RECIPROCAL = 591 = (59 x 1) = 59 = HEIGHT = 5' 9"!!!~'

AMERICAN ACTRESS LAUREN BACALL died at the AGE of 89!!!~'

BIRTHDAY # `-NUMBER = 9/16/19/24 = 9 + 16 + 19 + 24 = 68

BIRTH/DAY # `-NUMBER = 68 = RECIPROCAL = 86 = "FLIP EVERY (`-6) OVER to a (`-9)" = 89 = AGE of DEATH for AMERICAN ACTRESS LAUREN BACALL!!!~'

DEATHDAY # `-NUMBER = 8/12/20/14 = 8 + 12 + 20 + 14 = 54

BIRTH/DAY = 9/16 = (96 x 1) = 96 = (9 x 6) = 54 = DEATH/DAY # `-NUMBER!!!~'

(68 (-) 54) = 14 = (7 X 2) = 72 = (8 X 9) = AGE of DEATH for AMERICAN ACTRESS LAUREN BACALL!!!~'

(68 (-) 54) = 14 = (5 + 9) = HEIGHT = 5' 9"!!!~'

(68 + 54) = 122 = (1 + 22) = 23 = -a PROPHETIC # `-NUMBER = RECIPROCAL = 32 = FRAGMENTED BIRTH/DAY # `-NUMBER!!!~'

FRAGMENTED BIRTHDAY # `-NUMBER = 9 + 1 + 6 + 1 + 9 + 2 + 4 = 32

FRAGMENTED BIRTH/DAY # `-NUMBER = 32 = -a PROPHETIC # `-NUMBER!!!~'

FRAGMENTED DEATHDAY # `-NUMBER = 8 + 1 + 2 + 2 + 0 + 1 + 4 = 18

(32 (-) 18) = 14 = (7 X 2) = 72 = (8 X 9) = AGE of DEATH for AMERICAN ACTRESS LAUREN BACALL!!!~'

YEARS `-ACTIVE from 1942 to 2014 = 72 YEARS = (8 X 9) = 89 = AGE of DEATH for AMERICAN ACTRESS LAUREN BACALL!!!~'

BIRTH/YEAR = 19/24 = (19 + 24) = 43 = RECIPROCAL = 34

DEATH/YEAR = 20/14 = (20 + 14) = 34

(34 + 34) = 68 = BIRTH/DAY # `-NUMBER!!!~'

FROM BIRTH-TO-DEATH there are 35 DAYS!!!-'

(365 (-) 35) = 330 = (3 x 30) = 90 = DIED within HER 90th YEAR of EXISTENCE!!!~'

WAS `-BORN in the `-MONTH of (`-9); AND, `-DIED in the `-MONTH of (`-8) = 9/8 = RECIPROCAL = 89 = AGE of DEATH for AMERICAN ACTRESS LAUREN BACALL!!!~'

WAS `-MARRIED to JASON ROBARDS from 1961 TO 1969 = 8 YEARS!!!~'

WAS `-MARRIED to HUMPHREY BOGART from 1945 to 1957 = 12 YEARS!!!~'

YEARS `-MARRIED = (8/12) = DEATH/DAY!!!~'

DEATH/DAY = 8/12 = (8 – 1) (2) = 72 = (8 X 9) = AGE of DEATH for AMERICAN ACTRESS LAUREN BACALL!!!~'

BIRTH/YEAR = 19/24 = (1 x 9) (2 x 4) = 98 = RECIPROCAL = 89 = AGE of DEATH for AMERICAN ACTRESS LAUREN BACALL!!!~'

AMERICAN ACTRESS BETTY GRABLE (ELIZABETH RUTH GRABLE) died at the AGE of 56!!!~'

BIRTH/DAY # `-NUMBER = 65 = RECIPROCAL = 56 = AGE of DEATH for AMERICAN ACTRESS BETTY GRABLE (ELIZABETH RUTH GRABLE)!!!~'

BIRTHDAY # `-NUMBER = 12/18/19/16 = 12 + 18 + 19 + 16 = 65

BIRTH/DAY = 12/18 = (1 x 2) (1 – 8) = 2/7 = RECIPROCAL = 72 = DEATH/DAY!!!~'

DEATHDAY # `-NUMBER = 7/2/19/73 = 7 + 2 + 19 + 73 = 101

(101 + 65) = 166 = (16 x 6) = 96 = BIRTH/YEAR = 19/16) = (96 x 1 x 1) = 96

(101 (-) 65) = (`-36) = (18 x 2) = "SEE BELOW" for the FRAGMENTED BIRTH/DEATH DAY # `-NUMBERS!!!~'

FRAGMENTED BIRTHDAY # `-NUMBER = 1 + 2 + 1 + 8 + 1 + 9 + 1 + 6 = 29

FRAGMENTED DEATHDAY # `-NUMBER = 7 + 2 + 1 + 9 + 7 + 3 = 29

BIRTH/MONTH = JULY = 31 DAYS!!!~'

(31 (-) 2) – (DAY of BIRTH) = 29

FRAGMENTED BIRTH/DAY # `-NUMBER = 29 = FRAGMENTED DEATH/DAY # `-NUMBER = 29!!!~'

(`-29) = 2 x 9 = 18 (X TIMES) (`-2) = (`-36) = "SEE `-ABOVE"!!!~'

DEATH/YEAR = 19/73 = (19 + 73) = 92 = RECIPROCAL = 29

STARTED `-BEING `-ACTIVE in 19(29)!!!~'

YEARS `-ACTIVE from 19(29) TO 1973 = 44 YEARS = (4 x 4) = 16 = BIRTH/YEAR!!!~'

FROM BIRTH-TO-DEATH there are 169 DAYS = (1 – 6) (9) = 59 = "FLIP EVERY ('-9) OVER to a ('-6)" = 56 = AGE of DEATH for AMERICAN ACTRESS BETTY GRABLE (ELIZABETH RUTH GRABLE)!!!~'

(365 (-) 169) = 196 = (96 x 1) = 96 = (9 x 6) = 54 = DEATH/YEAR = 19/73 = (73 (-) 19) = 54 = HEIGHT 5' 4"!!!~'

WAS `-MARRIED to HARRY JAMES from 1943 TO 1965 = 22 YEARS!!!~'

WAS `-MARRIED to JACKIE COOGAN from 19(37) to 1939 = 2 YEARS!!!~'

YEARS `-MARRIED = 22/2 = (22 x 2) = YEARS `-ACTIVE = ('-44)!!!~'

YEARS `-MARRIED = 22/2 = "FLIP EVERY ('-2) OVER to a ('-7)" = 77/2 = DEATH/DAY!!!~'

`-FIRST `-MARRIED in ('-37) = RECIPROCAL = ('-73) = DEATH/YEAR!!!~'

BIRTH/DAY = 12/18 = (12 x 18) = 216 / (DIVIDED by) ('-3) = DEATH/DAY = 7/2!!!~'

BIRTH/YEAR = 19/16 = (1 x 9) (1 – 6) = 95 = RECIPROCAL = 59 = "FLIP EVERY ('-9) OVER to a ('-6)" = 56 = AGE of DEATH for AMERICAN ACTRESS BETTY GRABLE (ELIZABETH RUTH GRABLE)!!!~'

DEATH/YEAR = 19/73 = (9) (1 + 7 – 3) = 95 = RECIPROCAL = 59 = "FLIP EVERY ('-9) OVER to a ('-6)" = 56 = AGE of DEATH for AMERICAN ACTRESS BETTY GRABLE (ELIZABETH RUTH GRABLE)!!!~'

APPLES' STEVE JOBS (STEVEN PAUL JOBS) died at the AGE of 56!!!~'

BIRTH/DAY # `-NUMBER in `-REVERSE = (55 (-) 19 (-) 24 (-) 2) = 10 = MONTH of `-DEATH & FRAGMENTED DEATH/DAY # `-NUMBER = 10!!!~

BIRTH/DAY # `-NUMBER = 2/24/19/55 = 2 + 24 + 19 + 55 = 100

DEATHDAY # `-NUMBER = 10/5/20/11 = 10 + 5 + 20 + 11 = 46

(100 + 46) = 146 = (1 + 4) (6) = 56 = AGE of DEATH for APPLES' STEVE JOBS (STEVEN PAUL JOBS)!!!~'

(100 (-) 46) = 54 = (5 x 4) = 20 = WAS `-MARRIED to LAURENE POWELL JOBS for 20 YEARS!!!~'

DEATH/DAY = 10/5 = (10 x 5) = 50 (X TIMES) (`-2) = 100 = BIRTH/DAY # `-NUMBER!!!~'

FRAGMENTED BIRTHDAY # `-NUMBER = 2 + 2 + 4 + 1 + 9 + 5 + 5 = 28

FRAGMENTED BIRTH/DAY # `-NUMBER = 28 (X TIMES) (`-2) = 56 = AGE of DEATH for APPLES' STEVE JOBS (STEVEN PAUL JOBS)!!!~'

FRAGMENTED DEATHDAY # `-NUMBER = 1 + 0 + 5 + 2 + 0 + 1 + 1 = 10

FRAGMENTED DEATH/DAY # `-NUMBER = 10 = JUST `-ADD a `-ZERO = 100 = BIRTH/DAY # `-NUMBER!!!~'

$(28 + 10) = 38 = (3 \times 8) = 24 = RECIPROCAL = 42 = DAYS$ from BIRTH-TO-DEATH $= 142 = (42 \times 1) = 42 = RECIPROCAL = 24 =$ DAY of BIRTH!!!~'

FROM BIRTH-TO-DEATH there were 142 DAYS $= (14 \times 2) = 28 =$ FRAGMENTED BIRTH/DAY # `-NUMBER!!!~'

$(365 (-) 142) = 223 = (2 \times 23) = 46 = DEATH/DAY$ # `-NUMBER!!!~'

WAS `-BORN in the `-MONTH of (`-2); AND, `-DIED in the `-MONTH of (`-10) $= 2/10 = 2(10's) = 10/10 = (10 \times 10) = 100 =$ BIRTH/DAY # `-NUMBER!!!~'

WAS `-BORN in the `-MONTH of (`-2); AND, `-DIED in the `-MONTH of (`-10) $= 2/10 = (2 \times 10) = 20 = WAS$ `-MARRIED to LAURENE POWELL JOBS from 1991 TO 2011 for 20 YEARS!!!~'

BIRTH/YEAR $= 19/55 = (1 + 9 + 5) (5) = (15) (5) = (1 + 5) (5) = 65$ $= RECIPROCAL = 56 = AGE$ of DEATH for APPLES' STEVE JOBS (STEVEN PAUL JOBS)!!!~'

AMERICAN ACTOR LEONARD SIMON NIMOY (STAR TREK) died at the AGE of 83!!!~'

BIRTHDAY # `-NUMBER $= 3/26/19/31 = 3 + 26 + 19 + 31 = 79$

$79 = RECIPROCAL = 97$

$(97 + 79) = 176 /$ (DIVIDED by) (`-2) $= 88 =$ "FLIP EVERY (`-8) OVER to a (`-3)" $= 83 = AGE$ of DEATH for AMERICAN ACTOR LEONARD SIMON NIMOY!!!~'

DEATHDAY # `-NUMBER $= 2/27/20/15 = 2 + 27 + 20 + 15 = 64$

'-AGE of '-DEATH = ('-83) = (8 x 3) = 24 = DEATH/DAY #
'-NUMBER = 64 = (6 x 4) = 24

(79 + 64) = 143 = (1 + 43) = 44 = FRAG BIRTH/DEATH DAYS
'-ADDED '-UP '-TOGETHER!!!~'

(79 (-) 64) = 15 = DEATH/YEAR!!!~'

BIRTH/DAY = 3/26 = (3 + 26) = 29

DEATH/DAY = 2/27 = (2 + 27) = 29

BIRTH/DAY # '-NUMBER = 79 = "FLIP EVERY ('-7) OVER to a
('-2)" = 29

BIRTH/DAY = 3/26 (+) DEATH/DAY = 2/27 /|\ (3 + 26 + 2 + 27)
= 58 = RECIPROCAL = 85

BIRTH/YEAR = 19/31 (+) DEATH/YEAR = 20/15 /|\ (19 + 31 +
20 + 15) = 85

FRAGMENTED BIRTHDAY # '-NUMBER = 3 + 2 + 6 + 1 + 9 + 3
+ 1 = 25

DEATH/YEAR = **2**(01)**5**

FRAGMENTED DEATHDAY # '-NUMBER = 2 + 2 + 7 + 2 + 0 +
1 + 5 = 19

(25 + 19) = 44 = "SEE '-ABOVE"!!!~'

51 = RECIPROCAL = 15

YEARS '-ACTIVE from 1951 TO 2015 = 64 = DEATH/DAY #
'-NUMBER!!!~'

FROM BIRTH-TO-DEATH there are 27 DAYS = DAY of DEATH = 27th!!!~'

(365 (-) 27) = 338 = RECIPROCAL = 8/33 = AGE of DEATH for AMERICAN ACTOR LEONARD SIMON NIMOY!!!~'

BIRTH/YEAR = 19/31 = (1 – 9) (3 x 1) = 83 = AGE of DEATH for AMERICAN ACTOR LEONARD SIMON NIMOY!!!~'

WAS `-MARRIED to SUSAN BAY from 1989 TO 2015 = 26 YEARS!!!~'

WAS `-MARRIED to SANDRA ZOBER from 1954 to 1987 = 33 YEARS!!!~'

YEARS `-MARRIED = 26/33 = (2 + 6) (33) = 8/33 = AGE of DEATH for AMERICAN ACTOR LEONARD SIMON NIMOY!!!~'

AMERICAN ACTOR JACKSON DEFOREST KELLEY (STAR TREK) died at the AGE of 79!!!~'

BIRTHDAY # `-NUMBER = 1/20/19/20 = 1 + 20 + 19 + 20 = 60

BIRTH/DAY # `-NUMBER = 60 = (6 x 10) = (6 + 10) = 16 = RECIPROCAL = 61 = DEATH/DAY = 6/11!!!~'

BIRTH/DAY = 1/20 = (1 – 20) = 19 (+) DAY of BIRTH /|\ 20 = BIRTH/YEAR!!!~'

DEATHDAY # `-NUMBER = 6/11/19/99 = 6 + 11 + 19 + 99 = 135

DEATHDAY # `-NUMBER = 135 = (1 + 3) (5) = 45 = RECIPROCAL = 54 = MARRIED for this MANY YEARS!!!~'

FRAGMENTED BIRTHDAY # `-NUMBER = 1 + 2 + 0 + 1 + 9 + 2 + 0 = 15

HEIGHT = 5' 10" = (5 + 10) = 15 = RECIPROCAL = 51 = YEARS `-ACTIVE from 1947 TO 1998 = 51 YEARS = DEATH/DAY = 6/11 = (6 – 1) (1) = 51!!!~'

FRAGMENTED DEATHDAY # `-NUMBER = 6 + 1 + 1 + 1 + 9 + 9 + 9 = 36

FRAGMENTED DEATH/DAY # `-NUMBER = 36 = RECIPROCAL = 63 = (7 X 9) = AGE of DEATH for AMERICAN ACTOR JACKSON DEFOREST KELLEY!!!~'

DEATH/DAY # `-NUMBER in `-REVERSE = (99 (-) 19 (-) 11 (-) 6) = 63 = (7 X 9) = AGE of DEATH for AMERICAN ACTOR JACKSON DEFOREST KELLEY!!!~'

(36 + 15) = 51 = "SEE `-ABOVE"!!!~'

FROM BIRTH-TO-DEATH there are 142 DAYS = (14 + 2) = 16 = (7 + 9) = AGE of DEATH for AMERICAN ACTOR JACKSON DEFOREST KELLEY!!!~'

(365 (-) 142) = 223 = (22 x 3) = 66 = DEATH/DAY = 6/11 = (6 x 11) = 66!!!~'

WAS `-MARRIED to CAROLYN DOWLING from 1945 TO 1999 = 54 YEARS = RECIPROCAL = 45 = WAS `-MARRIED in (`-45)!!!~'

WAS `-BORN in the `-MONTH of (`-1); AND, `-DIED in the `-MONTH of (`-6) = 1/6 = RECIPROCAL = 61 = DEATH/DAY = 6/11!!!~'

BIRTH/MONTH = JANUARY = 31 DAYS!!!~'

(31 (-) 20) – (DAY of BIRTH) = 11 = DAY of `-DEATH!!!~'

CANADIAN ACTOR JAMES MONTGOMERY DOOHAN (STAR TREK) died at the AGE of 85!!!~'

BIRTHDAY # `-NUMBER = 3/(3/19)/20 = 3 + 3 + 19 + 20 = 45

(3/19) = SWIPE 1 = DIED (`-139) DAYS from BIRTH-TO-DEATH!!!~'

BIRTH/YEAR = 20 = DAY of `-DEATH = 20!!!~'

DEATHDAY # `-NUMBER = 7/20/20/05 = 7 + 20 + 20 + 05 = 52

(45 + 52) = 97 = RECIPROCAL = 79 = AGE of DEATH for AMERICAN ACTOR JACKSON DEFOREST KELLEY (STAR TREK)!!!~'

BIRTH/DAY = 3/3 (+) DEATH/DAY = 7/20 /|\ (3 + 3 + 7 + 20) = 3/3 = BIRTH/DAY!!!~'

DEATH/DAY = 7/20 = (7 – 20) = 13 = (8 + 5) = AGE of DEATH for CANADIAN ACTOR JAMES MONTGOMERY DOOHAN!!!~'

FRAGMENTED BIRTHDAY # `-NUMBER = 3 + 3 + 1 + 9 + 2 + 0 = 18

FRAGMENTED DEATHDAY # `-NUMBER = 7 + 2 + 0 + 2 + 0 + 0 + 5 = 16

(18 x 16) = 288 = (2 + 88) = 90 / (DIVIDED by) (`-2) = 45 = BIRTH/DAY # `-NUMBER!!!~'

(18/16) = (1 x 8) (1 – 6) = 85 = AGE of DEATH for CANADIAN ACTOR JAMES MONTGOMERY DOOHAN!!!~'

FROM BIRTH-TO-DEATH there were 139 DAYS = (1 x 39) = 39 = BIRTH/YEAR = (19 + 20) = 39!!!~'

DEATH/DAY = 7/20 = (7 + 20) = 27 = (3 X 9)!!!~'

FROM BIRTH-TO-DEATH there were 139 DAYS = (1 – 39) = 38 = YEARS of SERVICE in the CANADIAN ARMY STARTED in 38 and went to 45 = BIRTH/DAY # `-NUMBER!!!~'

(365 (-) 139) = 226 = (2 x 26) = 52 = DEATH/DAY # `-NUMBER!!!~'

52 = RECIPROCAL = 25 = DEATH/YEAR = (20 + 05) = 25

YEARS `-ACTIVE were from 19(52) TO (2)00(5) = 53 YEARS = RECIPROCAL = 35 = "FLIP EVERY ('-3) OVER to an ('-8)" = 85 = AGE of DEATH for CANADIAN ACTOR JAMES MONTGOMERY DOOHAN (STAR TREK)!!!~'

AMERICAN PROFESSIONAL BASEBALL PLAYER JACK ROOSEVELT ROBINSON died at the AGE of 53!!!~'

DEATH/YEAR = 19/72 = (72 (-) 19) = 53 = AGE of DEATH for AMERICAN PROFESSIONAL BASEBALL PLAYER JACK ROOSEVELT ROBINSON!!!~'

BIRTHDAY # `-NUMBER = 1/31/19/19 = 1 + 31 + 19 + 19 = 70

BIRTH/DAY # `-NUMBER = 70 / (DIVIDED by) ('-2) = 35 = RECIPROCAL = 53 = AGE of DEATH for AMERICAN

PROFESSIONAL BASEBALL PLAYER JACK ROOSEVELT ROBINSON!!!~'

PART of DEATH = (10 + 24 + 19) = 53 = AGE of DEATH for AMERICAN PROFESSIONAL BASEBALL PLAYER JACK ROOSEVELT ROBINSON!!!~'

DEATHDAY # `-NUMBER = (10/24/19)/72 = 10 + 24 + 19 + 72 = 125

(125 (-) 70) = 55 = (5 x 5) = 25 = FRAGMENTED BIRTH/DAY # `-NUMBER!!!~'

(125 + 70) = 195 = RECIPROCAL = 591 = (5) (9 − 1) = 58 = RECIPROCAL = 85

BROKE the BASEBALL COLOR LINE for WHEN STARTING at FIRST BASE for the BROOKLYN DODGERS on 4/15/19/47 = (4 + 15 + 19 + 47) = 85 = RECIPROCAL = 58 = "FLIP EVERY (`-8) OVER to a (`-3) = 53 = AGE of DEATH for AMERICAN PROFESSIONAL BASEBALL PLAYER JACK ROOSEVELT ROBINSON!!!~'

(4/15) = RECIPROCAL = 51/4 = (5) (1 − 4) = 53 = AGE of DEATH for AMERICAN PROFESSIONAL BASEBALL PLAYER JACK ROOSEVELT ROBINSON!!!~'

(19/47) = 19 + 47 = (`-66) = "SEE `-BELOW"!!!~'

DEATH/DAY # `-NUMBER = 125 = RECIPROCAL = 521 = (52 + 1) = 53 = AGE of DEATH for AMERICAN PROFESSIONAL BASEBALL PLAYER JACK ROOSEVELT ROBINSON!!!~'

DEATH/YEAR = 19/72 = (19 + 72) = 91 = RECIPROCAL = 19 = BIRTH/YEAR!!!~'

FRAGMENTED BIRTHDAY # `-NUMBER = 1 + 3 + 1 + 1 + 9 + 1 + 9 = 25

FRAGMENTED BIRTH/DAY # `-NUMBER = 25 = DEATH/DAY # `-NUMBER = 125 = (1 x 25) = 25!!!~'

FRAGMENTED DEATHDAY # `-NUMBER = 1 + 0 + 2 + 4 + 1 + 9 + 7 + 2 = 26

FRAGMENTED DEATH/DAY # `-NUMBER = 26 = WAS `-MARRIED to RACHEL ROBINSON from 1946 TO 1972 = 26 YEARS!!!~'

(25 + 26) = 51 = RECIPROCAL = 15

(51 + 15) = 66 = "SEE `-ABOVE & `-BELOW"!!!~'

BIRTH/YEAR = 19/19 = (99 x 1 x 1) = 99 = "SEE `-BELOW"!!!~'

FROM BIRTH-TO-DEATH there were 99 DAYS = "FLIP EVERY (`-9) OVER to a (`-6)" = 66 = BIRTH/DAY 1/31 (+) DEATH/DAY 10/24 /|\ (1 + 31 + 10 + 24) = 66 = 2(6's) = 26 = FRAGMENTED DEATH/DAY # `-NUMBER!!!~'

(365 (-) 99) = 266 = (2 x 66) = 132 = (1 x 32) = 32 = BIRTH/DAY = 1/31 = (1 + 31) = 32!!!~'

BROOKLYN DODGERS `-NUMBER = 42!!!~'

BIRTH/YEAR = 19/19 = (19 + 19) = 38 = (3 x 8) = 24 = DAY of DEATH = RECIPROCAL = 42!!!~'

BIRTH/DAY = 1/31 = (1 + 31) = 32

DEATH/DAY = 10/24 = HALF RECIPROCAL = 10/42 = (10 – 42) = 32

\-

AMERICAN PROFESSIONAL BASEBALL PLAYER MICKEY CHARLES MANTLE died at the AGE of 63!!!~'

BIRTHDAY # `-NUMBER = 10/20/1931 = 10 + 20 + 19 + 31 = 80

BIRTHDAY # `-NUMBER = 80 = (8 x 10) = (8 + 10) = 18 = (6 X 3) = AGE of DEATH for AMERICAN PROFESSIONAL BASEBALL PLAYER MICKEY CHARLES MANTLE!!!~'

PARTIAL DEATH/DAY # `-NUMBER in `-REVERSE = (95 (-) 19 (-) 13) = (`-63) = AGE of DEATH for AMERICAN PROFESSIONAL BASEBALL PLAYER MICKEY CHARLES MANTLE!!!~'

DEATHDAY # `-NUMBER = 8/13/19/95 = 8 + 13 + 19 + 95 = 135

DEATHDAY # `-NUMBER = 135 = RECIPROCAL = 531 = (5 + 1) (3) = 63 = AGE of DEATH for AMERICAN PROFESSIONAL BASEBALL PLAYER MICKEY CHARLES MANTLE!!!~'

(135 + 80) = 215 = (2 + 1) (5) = 35 = DEATH/DAY # `-NUMBER = 135 = (1 x 35) = 35

(135 + 80) = 215 = (2 x 15) = 30 = BIRTH/DAY = 10/20 = (10 + 20) = 30

BIRTH/DAY = 10/20 = HALF RECIPROCAL = 01/20 = (01 + 20) = 21

DEATH/DAY = 8/13 = (8 + 13) = 21

$(21 + 21) = 42 = DEATH/YEAR = 19/95 = (19 - 95) = 76 = (7 \times 6) = 42$

$DEATH/DAY = 8/13 = (8) (1 \times 3) = 83 = BIRTH/YEAR = 19/31 = (1 - 9) (3 \times 1) = 83$

$DEATH/YEAR = 19/95 = (95 (-) 19) = 76 / (DIVIDED$ by$) ('-2) = 38 = RECIPROCAL = 83$

$BIRTH/YEAR = 19/31 = (1 \times 9) (3 \times 1) = 93 =$ "FLIP EVERY $('-9)$ OVER to a $('-6)$" $= 63 = AGE$ of DEATH for AMERICAN PROFESSIONAL BASEBALL PLAYER MICKEY CHARLES MANTLE!!!~'

FRAGMENTED BIRTHDAY # '-NUMBER $= 1 + 0 + 2 + 0 + 1 + 9 + 3 + 1 = 17$

FRAGMENTED DEATHDAY # '-NUMBER $= 8 + 1 + 3 + 1 + 9 + 9 + 5 = 36$

FRAGMENTED DEATH/DAY # '-NUMBER = 36 = RECIPROCAL $= 63 = AGE$ of DEATH for AMERICAN PROFESSIONAL BASEBALL PLAYER MICKEY CHARLES MANTLE!!!~'

$(17 + 36) = 53 = RECIPROCAL = 35 = DEATH/DAY$ # '-NUMBER $= 135 = (35 \times 1) = 35$

FROM BIRTH-TO-DEATH there are $= 68$ DAYS $=$ "FLIP EVERY $('-8)$ OVER to a $('-3)$" $= 63 = AGE$ of DEATH for AMERICAN PROFESSIONAL BASEBALL PLAYER MICKEY CHARLES MANTLE!!!~'

$(365 (-) 68) = 297 = (29 + 7) = 36 = RECIPROCAL = 63 = AGE$ of DEATH for AMERICAN PROFESSIONAL BASEBALL PLAYER MICKEY CHARLES MANTLE!!!~'

DEATH/MONTH = AUGUST = 31 DAYS!!!~'

(31 (-) 13 – (DAY of DEATH) = 18 = (6 X 3) = AGE of DEATH for AMERICAN PROFESSIONAL BASEBALL PLAYER MICKEY CHARLES MANTLE!!!~'

BIRTH/YEAR = 31 = RECIPROCAL = 13 = DAY of DEATH!!!~'

(31 + 13) = ('-44)!!!~'

WAS '-MARRIED to MERLYN MANTLE from 19(51) TO 1995 = ('-44) YEARS!!!~'

WAS '-MARRIED in ('-51) = BIRTH/DAY 10/20 (+) DEATH/DAY 8/13 /|\ (10 + 20 + 8 + 13) = ('-51)!!!~'

WAS '-BORN in the '-MONTH of ('-10); AND, '-DIED in the '-MONTH of ('-8) = 10/8 = (10 + 8) = 18 = (6 X 3) = 63 = AGE of DEATH for AMERICAN PROFESSIONAL BASEBALL PLAYER MICKEY CHARLES MANTLE!!!~'

AMERICAN PROFESSIONAL BASEBALL PLAYER GEORGE HERMAN (BABE) RUTH JR. died at the AGE of 53!!!~'

BIRTH/DAY # '-NUMBER in '-REVERSE = (95 (-) 18 (-) 6 (-) 2) = 69 = DEATH/DAY = 8/16 = (8 + 1) (6) = 96 = RECIPROCAL = 69!!!~'

BIRTH/DAY # '-NUMBER in '-REVERSE = (95 (-) 18 (-) 6 (-) 2) = 69 = DEATH/DAY = 8/16 = RECIPROCAL = 61/8 = (61 + 8) = 69!!!~'

BIRTHDAY # '-NUMBER = 2/6/18/95 = 2 + 6 + 18 + 95 = 121

BIRTH/DAY = 2/6 = (2 + 6) = 8 = (5 + 3) = AGE of DEATH for AMERICAN PROFESSIONAL BASEBALL PLAYER GEORGE HERMAN (BABE) RUTH JR.!!!~'

DEATHDAY # '-NUMBER = 8/16/19/48 = 8 + 16 + 19 + 48 = 91

DEATHDAY # '-NUMBER = 91 = (9 – 1) = 8 = (5 + 3) = AGE of DEATH for AMERICAN PROFESSIONAL BASEBALL PLAYER GEORGE HERMAN (BABE) RUTH JR.!!!~'

DEATH/DAY = 8/16 = (8 – 16) = 8 = (5 + 3) = AGE of DEATH for AMERICAN PROFESSIONAL BASEBALL PLAYER GEORGE HERMAN (BABE) RUTH JR.!!!~'

DEATH/DAY = 8/16 = HALF RECIPROCAL = 8/61 = (61 (-) 8) = 53 = AGE of DEATH for AMERICAN PROFESSIONAL BASEBALL PLAYER GEORGE HERMAN (BABE) RUTH JR.!!!~'

(121 + 91) = 212 = (2 x 12) = 24 = DEATH/DAY = 8/16 = (8 + 16) = 24

(24 + 24) = 48 = DEATH/YEAR!!!~'

BIRTH/YEAR = 18/95 = (18 + 95) = 113 = (1 x 13) = 13

DEATH/YEAR = 19/48 = (19 + 48) = 67 = (6 + 7) = 13

DEATH/DAY = 8/16 = RECIPROCAL = 61/8 = (6) (1 – 8) = 67 = DEATH/YEAR = 19/48 = (19 + 48) = 67

FRAGMENTED BIRTHDAY # '-NUMBER = 2 + 6 + 1 + 8 + 9 + 5 = 31

FRAGMENTED DEATHDAY # '-NUMBER = 8 + 1 + 6 + 1 + 9 + 4 + 8 = 37

(37 (-) 31) = 6 = DAY of BIRTH!!!~'

(31 + 37) = 68 = (6 x 8) = 48 = DEATH/YEAR!!!~'

DEATH/DAY = 8/16 = RECIPROCAL = 61/8 = (68 x 1) = 68

FROM BIRTH-TO-DEATH there are = 191 DAYS = (1 x 91) = 91 = DEATH/DAY # `-NUMBER!!!~'

(365 (-) 191) = 174 = (17 x 4) – 68 = FRAG BIRTH/DEATH DAYS `-ADDED `-UP `-TOGETHER = DEATH/DAY as WELL!!!~'

BIRTH/YEAR = 18/95 = (8) (1 + 9 – 5) = 85 = RECIPROCAL = 58 = "FLIP EVERY (`-8) OVER to a (`-3)" = 53 = AGE of DEATH for AMERICAN PROFESSIONAL BASEBALL PLAYER GEORGE HERMAN (BABE) RUTH JR.!!!~'

AMERICAN PROFESSIONAL BASEBALL PLAYER ROGER EUGENE MARIS died at the AGE of 51!!!~'

BIRTH/DAY = 9/10 = (9 x 10) = 90 / (DIVIDED by) (`-2) = 45 = BIRTH/DAY 9/10 (+) DEATH/DAY 12/14 /|\ (9 + 10 + 12 + 14) = 45!!!~'

BIRTHDAY # `-NUMBER = 9/10/19/34 = 9 + 10 + 19 + 34 = 72

DEATHDAY # `-NUMBER = 12/14/19/85 = 12 + 14 + 19 + 85 = 130

(130 (-) 72) = 58 = FLIP EVERY (`-8) OVER to a (`-3)" = 53 = BIRTH/YEAR = (19 + 34) = 53

DEATH/YEAR = 85 = RECIPROCAL = 58

BIRTH/YEAR = 19/34 = (19 + 34) = 53 = "FLIP EVERY (`-3) OVER to an (`-8)" = 58

DEATH/DAY = 12/14 = (12 x 14) = 168 = (1 – 6) (8) = 58

DEATH/YEAR = 19/85 = (1 + 9 + 8) (5) = (18) (5) = (1 x 8) (5) = 85 = RECIPROCAL = 58

DEATH/DAY # `-NUMBER = 130 = (13 + 0) = 13 = RECIPROCAL = 31 = FRAGMENTED DEATH/DAY # `-NUMBER!!!~'

FRAGMENTED BIRTHDAY # `-NUMBER = 9 + 1 + 0 + 1 + 9 + 3 + 4 = 27

FRAGMENTED DEATHDAY # `-NUMBER = 1 + 2 + 1 + 4 + 1 + 9 + 8 + 5 = 31

(27 + 31) = 58 = FLIP EVERY (`-8) OVER to a (`-3)" = 53 = BIRTH/YEAR = (19 + 34) = 53

DEATH/YEAR = 85 = RECIPROCAL = 58

DEATH/YEAR = 19/85 = (1 + 9 + 8) (5) = (18) (5) = (1 x 8) (5) = 85 = RECIPROCAL = 58

(`-56) = (5 + 6) = 11 /|\ (`-85) = (8 x 5) = 40

(40 + 11) = 51 = AGE of DEATH for AMERICAN PROFESSIONAL BASEBALL PLAYER ROGER EUGENE MARIS!!!~'

WAS `-MARRIED to PATRICIA A. MARIS from 19(56) TO 19(85) = 29 YEARS!!!~'

DEATH/DAY # `-NUMBER = 130 = (1 – 30) = 29!!!~'

WAS `-BORN in the `-MONTH of (`-9); AND, `-DIED in the `-MONTH of (`-12) = 9/12 = (92 x 1) = 92 = RECIPROCAL = 29!!!~'

FROM BIRTH-TO-DEATH there were 95 DAYS = RECIPROCAL = 59 = "FLIP EVERY (`-9) OVER to a (`-6)" = 56 = WAS `-MARRIED in (`-56)!!!~'

DEATH/DAY # `-NUMBER = 130 / (DIVIDED by) (`-2) = 65 = RECIPROCAL = (`-56)!!!~'

(365 (-) 95) = 270 = (27 + 0) = 27 = FRAGMENTED BIRTH/DAY # `-NUMBER = RECIPROCAL = 72 = BIRTH/DAY # `-NUMBER!!!~'

HAD HOME RUN RECORD of 19(61) of HITTING (`-61) HOME RUNS in a SINGLE SEASON!!!~'

(19/61) = (1 + 9) (61) = (10) (61) = (61 (-) 10) = 51 = AGE of DEATH for AMERICAN PROFESSIONAL BASEBALL PLAYER ROGER EUGENE MARIS!!!~'

BIRTH/YEAR = 19/34 = "FLIP EVERY (`-9) OVER to a (`-6)" = 16/34 = (1 – 6) (3 – 4) = 51 = AGE of DEATH for AMERICAN PROFESSIONAL BASEBALL PLAYER ROGER EUGENE MARIS!!!~'

AMERICAN PROFESSIONAL BASEBALL PLAYER JOSEPH PAUL DIMAGGIO died at the AGE of 84!!!~'

DEATH/DAY # `-NUMBER in REVERSE = (99 (-) 19 (-) 8 (-) 3) = 69 = BIRTHDAY # `-NUMBER = 69!!!~'

BIRTH/YEAR = 19/14 = (19 + 14) = 33 (X TIMES ('-3) = 99 = DEATH/YEAR!!!~'

BIRTHDAY # '-NUMBER = 11/25/19/14 = 11 + 25 + 19 + 14 = 69

DEATHDAY # '-NUMBER = 3/8/19/99 = 3 + 8 + 19 + 99 = 129

(69 + 129) = 198 = (1 + 98) = 99 = DEATH/YEAR!!!~'

DEATH/DAY # '-NUMBER = 129 = "FLIP EVERY ('-2) OVER to a ('-7)" = 179 = (1 – 7) (9) = 69 = BIRTH/DAY # '-NUMBER!!!~'

BIRTH/DAY = 11/25 = (11 + 25) = 36 = "FLIP EVERY ('-6) OVER to a ('-9)" = 39 = DEATH/DAY # '-NUMBER = 129 = (1 + 2) (9) = 39 = FRAGMENTED DEATH/DAY # '-NUMBER = 39!!!~'

BIRTH/DAY = 11/25 = (11 + 25) = 36 = "FLIP EVERY ('-6) OVER to a ('-9)" = 39 = FRAGMENTED DEATH/DAY # '-NUMBER = 39!!!~'

DEATH/YEAR = 1999 = (1) (999) = (1 x 999) = 999 = 3(9's) = ('-39)!!!~'

FRAGMENTED BIRTHDAY # '-NUMBER = 1 + 1 + 2 + 5 + 1 + 9 + 1 + 4 = 24

FRAGMENTED BIRTH/DAY # '-NUMBER = 24 = (3 x 8) = DEATH/DAY!!!~'

FRAGMENTED DEATHDAY # '-NUMBER = 3 + 8 + 1 + 9 + 9 + 9 = 39

FRAGMENTED DEATH/DAY # '-NUMBER = 39 = (3 x 9) = 27 = BIRTH/DAY = 11/25 = (1 + 1) (25) = (2) (25) = (2 + 25) = 27

(27 + 27) = 54 = (6 X 9) = BIRTH/DAY # `-NUMBER!!!~'

(24 + 39) = 63 = "FLIP EVERY (`-3) OVER to an (`-8)" = 68 = (6 x 8) = 48 = RECIPROCAL = 84 = AGE of DEATH for AMERICAN PROFESSIONAL BASEBALL PLAYER JOSEPH PAUL DIMAGGIO!!!~'

BIRTH/DAY = 11/25 = (11 + 25) = 36 = RECIPROCAL = 63

DEATH/MONTH = AUGUST = 31 DAYS!!!~'

(31 (-) 8) – (DAY of DEATH) = (`-23) = -a PROPHETIC # `-NUMBER!!!~'

(`-23) = RECIPROCAL = (`-32) = (8 X 4) = AGE of DEATH for AMERICAN PROFESSIONAL BASEBALL PLAYER JOSEPH PAUL DIMAGGIO!!!~'

FROM BIRTH-TO-DEATH there are = 103 DAYS = (10 + 3) = 13 = "A VERY PIVOTAL # `-NUMBER" = PLAYED ENTIRE (`-13) YEAR CAREER in MAJOR LEAGUE BASEBALL for the NEW YORK YANKEES!!!~'

WAS `-BORN in the `-MONTH of (`-11); AND, `-DIED in the `-MONTH of (`-3) = 11/3 = (13 x 1) = (`-13)!!!~'

(365 (-) 103) = 262 = (2 – 6) (2) = 42 (X TIMES) (`-2) = 84 = AGE of DEATH for AMERICAN PROFESSIONAL BASEBALL PLAYER JOSEPH PAUL DIMAGGIO!!!~'

WAS `-BORN in the `-MONTH of (`-11); AND, `-DIED in the `-MONTH of (`-3) = 11/3 = (11 x 3) = 33 = BIRTH/YEAR = (19 + 14) = 33!!!~'

BIRTH/YEAR = 19/14 = (1 – 9) (1 x 4) = 84 = AGE of DEATH for AMERICAN PROFESSIONAL BASEBALL PLAYER JOSEPH PAUL DIMAGGIO!!!~'

AMERICAN PROFESSIONAL BASEBALL PLAYER HENRY LOUIS AARON died at the AGE of 86!!!~'

BIRTHDAY # '-NUMBER = 2/5/19/34 = 2 + 5 + 19 + 34 = 60

DEATHDAY # '-NUMBER = 1/22/20/21 = 1 + 22 + 20 + 21 = 64

(60 + 64) = 124 = (1 x 24) = 24 = FRAGMENTED BIRTH/DAY # '-NUMBER = 24!!!~'

FRAGMENTED BIRTHDAY # '-NUMBER = 2 + 5 + 1 + 9 + 3 + 4 = 24

FRAGMENTED DEATHDAY # '-NUMBER = 1 + 2 + 2 + 2 + 0 + 2 + 1 = 10

(24 (-) 10) = 14 = DAYS from BIRTH-TO-DEATH!!!~'

FROM BIRTH-TO-DEATH there are 14 DAYS = (8 + 6) = AGE of DEATH for AMERICAN PROFESSIONAL BASEBALL PLAYER HENRY LOUIS AARON!!!~'

(365 (-) 14) = 351 = "FLIP EVERY ('-3) OVER to an ('-8)" = 851 = (8) (5 + 1) = 86 = AGE of DEATH for AMERICAN PROFESSIONAL BASEBALL PLAYER HENRY LOUIS AARON!!!~'

DEATH/DAY = 1/22 = (1 + 22) = 23 = PLAYED ('-23) YEARS in MAJOR LEAGUE BASEBALL from 1954 TO 1976!!!~'

BIRTH/MONTH = FEBRUARY = 28 DAYS!!!~'

(28 (-) 5) – (DAY of BIRTH) = ('-23) = DEATH/DAY = 1/22 = (1 + 22) = ('-23)!!!~'

BIRTH/YEAR = 19/34 = (9) (1 + 3 + 4) = 98 = RECIPROCAL = 89 = "FLIP EVERY ('-9) OVER to a ('-6)" = 86 = AGE of DEATH for AMERICAN PROFESSIONAL BASEBALL PLAYER HENRY LOUIS AARON!!!~'

WAS '-MARRIED to BILLYE AARON from 1973 TO 2021 = 48 YEARS = (8 X 6) = AGE of DEATH for AMERICAN PROFESSIONAL BASEBALL PLAYER HENRY LOUIS AARON!!!~'

WAS '-MARRIED to BARBARA LUCAS from 1953 TO 1971 = 18 YEARS = (6 X 3) = "FLIP EVERY ('-3) OVER to an ('-8)" = 68 = RECIPROCAL = 86 = AGE of DEATH for AMERICAN PROFESSIONAL BASEBALL PLAYER HENRY LOUIS AARON!!!~'

AMERICAN PROFESSIONAL BASEBALL PLAYER WILLIE LEE MCCOVEY died at the AGE of 80!!!~'

DEATH/DAY = 10/31 = "FLIP EVERY ('-3) OVER to an ('-8)" = 10/81 = HALF RECIPROCAL = 01/81 = (81 (-) 01) = 80 = AGE of DEATH for AMERICAN PROFESSIONAL BASEBALL PLAYER WILLIE LEE MCCOVEY!!!~'

BIRTH/YEAR = 38 = DEATH/YEAR = (20 + 18) = 38

BIRTHDAY # '-NUMBER = 1/10/19/38 = 1 + 10 + 19 + 38 = 68

BIRTH/DAY # `-NUMBER = 68 = "FLIP EVERY (`-8) OVER to a (`-3)" = 63 = (7 X 9) = DEATH/DAY # `-NUMBER!!!~'

(79 (-) 68) = 11 = BIRTH/DAY = 1/10 = (1 + 10) = 11

DEATHDAY # `-NUMBER = 10/31/20/18 = 10 + 31 + 20 + 18 = 79

DEATH/DAY = 10/31 = HALF RECIPROCAL = 10/13 = (10 + 13) = (`-23) = -a PROPHETIC # `-NUMBER!!!~'

FRAGMENTED BIRTHDAY # `-NUMBER = 1 + 1 + 0 + 1 + 9 + 3 + 8 = 23

FRAGMENTED DEATHDAY # `-NUMBER = 1 + 0 + 3 + 1 + 2 + 0 + 1 + 8 = 16

(23 (-) 16) = 7 = (7 x 1) = (`-71)!!!~'

FROM BIRTH-TO-DEATH there are = 71 DAYS = "FLIP EVERY (`-7) OVER to a (`-2)" = 21 = PLAYED in the MAJOR LEAGUE BASEBALL from 1959 TO 1980 = 21 YEARS!!!~'

(365 (-) 71) = 294 = "FLIP EVERY (`-9) OVER to a (`-6)" = 264 = (6) (2 x 4) = 68 = BIRTH/DAY # `-NUMBER!!!~'

BIRTH/YEAR = 19/38 = (38 (-) 19) = 19 = (1 – 9) = 8 = (8 + 0) = 80 = AGE of DEATH for AMERICAN PROFESSIONAL BASEBALL PLAYER WILLIE LEE MCCOVEY!!!~'

BIRTH/YEAR = 19/38 = (1 + 9 + 3 + 8) = 21 = "FLIP EVERY (`-2) OVER to a (`-7)" = 71 = DAYS from BIRTH-TO-DEATH!!!~'

ENGLISH MULTI-INSTRUMENTAL MUSICIAN IAN MCDONALD died at the AGE of 75!!!~'

BIRTHDAY # `-NUMBER = 6/25/19/46 = 6 + 25 + 19 + 46 = 96

DEATHDAY # `-NUMBER = 2/9/20/22 = 2 + 9 + 20 + 22 = 53

DEATH/DAY # `-NUMBER = 53 = BIRTH/DAY = 6/25 = (6 + 2) (5) = 85 = RECIPROCAL = 58 = "FLIP EVERY (`-8) OVER to a (`-3)" = 53

`-AGE of `-DEATH = (`-75) = (7 x 5) = 35 = RECIPROCAL = 53 = DEATH/DAY # `-NUMBER!!!~'

FRAGMENTED BIRTHDAY # `-NUMBER = 6 + 2 + 5 + 1 + 9 + 4 + 6 = 33

FRAGMENTED DEATHDAY # `-NUMBER = 2 + 9 + 2 + 0 + 2 + 2 = 17

(33/17) = RECIPROCAL = 71/33 = (7) (1 – 3 + 3) = 75 = AGE of DEATH for ENGLISH MULTI-INSTRUMENTAL MUSICIAN IAN MCDONALD!!!~'

(33 + 17) = 50 = BIRTH/DAY = 6/25 = (6 x 25) = 150 = (1 x 50) = 50

PART of BIRTH DAY = (6 + 25 + 19) = 50

FROM BIRTH-TO-DEATH there are 136 DAYS = "FLIP EVERY (`-3) OVER to an (`-8)" = 186 = (1 + 8) (6) = 96 = BIRTH/DAY # `-NUMBER!!!~'

(365 (-) 136) = 229 = (22 + 9) = 31 = BIRTH/DAY = 6/25 = (6 + 25) = 31

PART of DEATH DAY = (2 + 9 + 20) = 31

DAY of BIRTH = 25th = "FLIP EVERY ('-2) OVER to a ('-7)" = 75 = AGE of DEATH for ENGLISH MULTI-INSTRUMENTAL MUSICIAN IAN MCDONALD!!!~'

WAS '-BORN in the '-MONTH of ('-6); AND, '-DIED in the '-MONTH of ('-2) = 6/2 = RECIPROCAL = 2/6 = "FLIP EVERY ('-6) OVER to a ('-9)" = 2/9 = DEATH/DAY!!!~'

BIRTH/YEAR = 19/46 = (1 + 6) (9 – 4) = 75 = AGE of DEATH for ENGLISH MULTI-INSTRUMENTAL MUSICIAN IAN MCDONALD!!!~'

CZECHOSLOVAK-BORN CANADIAN FILM & TELEVISION DIRECTOR IVAN REITMAN died at the AGE of 75!!!~'

BIRTHDAY # '-NUMBER = 10/27/19/46 = 10 + 27 + 19 + 46 = 102

DEATH/DAY # '-NUMBER = 2/12/20/22 = 2 + 12 + 20 + 22 = 56

(102 + 56) = 158 = RECIPROCAL = 851 = (8 – 1) (5) = 75 = AGE of DEATH for CZECHOSLOVAK-BORN CANADIAN FILM & TELEVISION DIRECTOR IVAN REITMAN!!!~'

(102 (-) 56) = 46 = BIRTH/YEAR!!!~'

BIRTH/DAY = 10/27 = (10 + 27) = 37

DEATH/DAY = 2/12 = "FLIP EVERY ('-2) OVER to a ('-7)" = 2/17 = (2 + 1) (7) = 37

FRAGMENTED BIRTHDAY # '-NUMBER = 1 + 0 + 2 + 7 + 1 + 9 + 4 + 6 = 30

DEATH/DAY # `-NUMBER = 56 = (5 x 6) = 30 = FRAGMENTED
BIRTH/DAY # `-NUMBER = 30!!!~'

FRAGMENTED DEATHDAY # `-NUMBER = 2 + 1 + 2 + 2 + 0 +
2 + 2 = 11

(30 (-) 11) = 19 (X TIMES) (`-4) = 76 = DIED within `-HIS (`-76th)
YEAR of `-EXISTENCE!!!~'

DEATH/YEAR = 20/22 = (20 + 22) = 42 = (7 X 6)!!!~'

WAS `-MARRIED in (`-76)!!!~'

WAS `-MARRIED to GENEVIEVE ROBERT from 19(76) to (2022)
= 46 YEARS = BIRTH/YEAR = 46!!!~'

FROM BIRTH-TO-DEATH there were 108 DAYS = (10 + 8) = 18 =
FOUNDED THE MONTECITO PICTURE COMPANY in 1998
= (19 + 98) = 117 = (11 + 7) = 18!!!~'

(365 (-) 108) = 257 = (25 x 7) = 175 = (75 x 1) = 75 = AGE of DEATH for
CZECHOSLOVAK-BORN CANADIAN FILM & TELEVISION
DIRECTOR IVAN REITMAN!!!~'

BIRTH/YEAR = 19/46 = (1 + 6) (9 − 4) = 75 = AGE of DEATH for
CZECHOSLOVAK-BORN CANADIAN FILM & TELEVISION
DIRECTOR IVAN REITMAN!!!~'

AMERICAN ACTOR FREDERICK HUBBARD GWYNNE (THE
MUNSTERS) died at the AGE of 66!!!~'

BIRTH/DAY = 7/10 (+) DEATH/DAY = 7/2 /|\ (7 + 10 + 7 + 2) = 26 = 2(6's) = 66 = AGE of '-DEATH for AMERICAN ACTOR FREDERICK HUBBARD GWYNNE (THE MUNSTERS)!!!~'

BIRTHDAY # '--NUMBER = 7/10/19/26 = 7 + 10 + 19 + 26 = 62

BIRTHDAY # '-NUMBER = 62 = RECIPROCAL = 26 = BIRTHYEAR = 2(6's) = 66 = AGE of '-DEATH for AMERICAN ACTOR FREDERICK HUBBARD GWYNNE (THE MUNSTERS)!!!~'

DEATHDAY # '-NUMBER = 7/2/19/93 = 7 + 2 + 19 + 93 = 121

(121 (-) 62) = 59 = (5 x 9) = 45 = BIRTH/YEAR = (19 + 26) = 45!!!~'

(121 + 62) = 183 = (18 x 3) = 54 = RECIPROCAL = 45 = BIRTH/YEAR = (19 + 26) = 45!!!~'

FRAGMENTED BIRTHDAY # '-NUMBER = 7 + 1 + 0 + 1 + 9 + 2 + 6 = 26 = BIRTHYEAR = 2(6's) = 66 = AGE of '-DEATH for AMERICAN ACTOR FREDERICK HUBBARD GWYNNE (THE MUNSTERS)!!!~'

FRAGMENTED BIRTHDAY # '-NUMBER = 7 + 1 + 0 + 1 + 9 + 2 + 6 = 26 = RECIPROCAL = 62 = BIRTHDAY # '-NUMBER!!!~'

FRAGMENTED DEATHDAY # '-NUMBER = 7 + 2 + 1 + 9 + 9 + 3 = 31

FRAGMENTED DEATH/DAY # '-NUMBER = 31 = DEATH/DAY # '-NUMBER = 121 = (1 + 2) (1) = 31!!!~

(26 + 31) = 57 = (5 + 7) = 12 = (2 x 6) = ('-26) = 2(6's) = 66 = AGE of '-DEATH for AMERICAN ACTOR FREDERICK HUBBARD GWYNNE (THE MUNSTERS)!!!~'

HEIGHT was 6' 5"!!!~'

DEATH/DAY # '-NUMBER in '-REVERSE = (93 (-) 19 (-) 2 (-) 7) = ('-65)!!!~'

DEATH/YEAR = 19/93 = (19 + 93) = 112 / (DIVIDED by) ('-2) = 56 = RECIPROCAL = 65

WAS '-MARRIED to DEBORAH FLATER from 1988 TO 1993 = 5 YEARS!!!~'

WAS '-MARRIED to JEAN REYNARD from 1952 TO 1980 = 28 YEARS!!!~'

'-MARRIED for (5 + 28) = 33 (X TIMES) ('-2) = 66 = AGE of '-DEATH for AMERICAN ACTOR FREDERICK HUBBARD GWYNNE (THE MUNSTERS)!!!~'

FROM BIRTH-TO-DEATH there are ('-8) DAYS = (2 + 6) = 26 = 2(6's) = 66 = AGE of '-DEATH for AMERICAN ACTOR FREDERICK HUBBARD GWYNNE (THE MUNSTERS)!!!~'

(365 (-) 8) = 357 = (35 + 7) = 42 = (6 X 7) = DIED within '-HIS ('-67th) YEAR of EXISTENCE!!!~'

BIRTH/YEAR = 26 = 2(6's) = 66 = AGE of '-DEATH for AMERICAN ACTOR FREDERICK HUBBARD GWYNNE (THE MUNSTERS)!!!~'

BIRTH/YEAR = 19/26 = (1 – 9 – 2) (6) = 66 = AGE of '-DEATH for AMERICAN ACTOR FREDERICK HUBBARD GWYNNE (THE MUNSTERS)!!!~'

CANADIAN-AMERICAN ACTRESS YVONNE DE CARLO (MARGARET YVONNE MIDDLETON) (THE MUNSTERS) died at the AGE of 84!!!~'

BIRTH/DAY # `-NUMBER = 9/1/19/22 = 9 + 1 + 19 + 22 = 51

DEATHDAY # `-NUMBER = 1/8/20/07 = 1 + 8 + 20 + 07 = 36

(51/36) = (5) (1 – 3 – 6) = 54 = HEIGHT was 5' 4"!!!~'

BIRTH/DAY = 9/1 = (9 x 1) = 9

DEATH/DAY = 1/8 = (1 + 8) = 9

(9/9) = 2(9's) = "SEE `-BELOW"!!!~'

BIRTH/YEAR = (`-22) = "FLIP EVERY (`-2) OVER to a (`-7)" = (`-27) = DEATH/YEAR = (20 + 07) = (`-27)!!!~'

FRAGMENTED BIRTHDAY # `-NUMBER = 9 + 1 + 1 + 9 + 2 + 2 = 24

FRAGMENTED DEATHDAY # `-NUMBER = 1 + 8 + 2 + 0 + 0 + 7 = 18

FRAGMENTED DEATH/DAY # `-NUMBER = 18 = DEATH/DAY = 1/8!!!~'

(24 + 18) = 42 (X TIMES) (`-2) = 84 = AGE of `-DEATH for CANADIAN-AMERICAN ACTRESS YVONNE DE CARLO (MARGARET YVONNE MIDDLETON) (THE MUNSTERS)!!!~'

BIRTH/MONTH = SEPTEMBER = 30 DAYS!!!~'

(30 (-) 1) – (DAY of BIRTH) = 29

WAS `-MARRIED to BOB MORGAN from 1955 TO 1973 for 18 YEARS = 1/8 = DEATH/DAY = (2 x 9)!!!~'

FROM BIRTH-TO-DEATH there are 129 DAYS = (1 x 29) = 29!!!~'

(365 (-) 129) = 236 = (2) (3 + 6) = 29!!!~'

BIRTH/YEAR = 19/22 = (1 – 9) (2 + 2) = 84 = AGE of `-DEATH for CANADIAN-AMERICAN ACTRESS YVONNE DE CARLO (MARGARET YVONNE MIDDLETON) (THE MUNSTERS)!!!~'

WAS `-BORN in the `-MONTH of (`-9); AND, `-DIED in the `-MONTH of (`-1) = 9/1 = BIRTH/DAY!!!~'

AMERICAN ACTRESS BEVERLEY OWEN (THE MUNSTERS) died at the AGE of 81!!!~'

BIRTH/DAY = 5/13 = (5 + 13) = 18 = RECIPROCAL = 81 = AGE of DEATH for AMERICAN ACTRESS BEVERLEY OWEN (THE MUNSTERS)!!!~'

BIRTHDAY # `-NUMBER = 5/13/19/37 = 5 + 13 + 19 + 37 = 74

BIRTH/DAY # `-NUMBER = 74 = (7 x 4) = 28 = RECIPROCAL = 82 = DIED within HER (`-82nd) YEAR of EXISTENCE!!!~'

DEATHDAY # `-NUMBER = 2/21/20/19 = 2 + 21 + 20 + 19 = 62

DEATH/DAY # `-NUMBER = 62 = RECIPROCAL = 26 = 2(6's) = 66 = "FLIP EVERY (`-6) OVER to a (`-9)" = 99 = (9 x 9) = 81 = AGE of DEATH for AMERICAN ACTRESS BEVERLEY OWEN (THE MUNSTERS)!!!~'

$(74 + 62) = 136 = (36 \times 1) = 36 = (6 \times 6) = $ "FLIP EVERY (`-6) OVER to a (`-9)" $= (9 \times 9) = 81 = $ AGE of DEATH for AMERICAN ACTRESS BEVERLEY OWEN (THE MUNSTERS)!!!~'

DAY of `-BIRTH $= 13^{th} = $ "FLIP EVERY (`-3) OVER to an (`-8)" $= 18 = $ RECIPROCAL $= 81 = $ AGE of DEATH for AMERICAN ACTRESS BEVERLEY OWEN (THE MUNSTERS)!!!~'

FRAGMENTED BIRTHDAY # `-NUMBER $= 5 + 1 + 3 + 1 + 9 + 3 + 7 = 29$

FRAGMENTED BIRTH/DAY # `-NUMBER $= 29 = 2(9's) = 99 = (9 \times 9) = 81 = $ AGE of DEATH for AMERICAN ACTRESS BEVERLEY OWEN (THE MUNSTERS)!!!~'

FRAGMENTED BIRTH/DAY # `-NUMBER $= 29 = $ "FLIP EVERY (`-9) OVER to a (`-6)" $= 26 = $ RECIPROCAL $= 62 = $ DEATH/DAY # `-NUMBER!!!~'

FRAGMENTED BIRTH/DAY # `-NUMBER $= 29 = $ DEATH/YEAR $= 20/19 = (2 + 0) (1 \times 9) = 29!!!~'$

FRAGMENTED DEATHDAY # `-NUMBER $= 2 + 2 + 1 + 2 + 0 + 1 + 9 = 17$

$(29 + 17) = 46 = $ (`-23) X (`-2) $= $ Reciprocal-Sequencing-Numerology-RSN $= $ DEATH/DAY $= 2/21 = (2 + 21) = $ (`-23)!!!~'

(`-46) $= $ RECIPROCAL $= $ (`-64) $= $ WAS `-MARRIED in (`-64)!!!~'

ENDED `-MARRIAGE in (`-74) $= $ BIRTH/DAY # `-NUMBER $= $ (`-74)!!!~'

WAS `-MARRIED to JON STONE from 19(64) TO 19(74) $= 10$ YEARS!!!~'

WAS `-BORN in the `-MONTH of (`-5); AND, `-DIED in the `-MONTH of (`-2) = (5/2) = (5 x 2) = 10 = WAS `-MARRIED for (`-10) `-YEARS!!!~'

BIRTH/DAY = 5/13 = (5) (1 – 3) = (`-52)!!!~'

FROM BIRTH-TO-DEATH there were (`-81) DAYS = AGE of DEATH (`-81) for AMERICAN ACTRESS BEVERLEY OWEN (THE MUNSTERS)!!!~'

(365 (-) 81) = 284 = (2 – 84) = 82 = DIED within HER (`-82nd) YEAR of EXISTENCE!!!~'

BIRTH/YEAR = 19/37 = (1 – 9) (3 + 7) = (8) (10) = (8 + 10) = 18 = RECIPROCAL = 81 = AGE of DEATH for AMERICAN ACTRESS BEVERLEY OWEN (THE MUNSTERS)!!!~'

AMERICAN ACTOR AL LEWIS (THE MUNSTERS) died at the AGE of 82!!!~'

BIRTH/YEAR = (`-23) = DEATH/DAY = (2/3)!!!~'

BIRTHDAY # `-NUMBER = 4/30/19/23 = 4 + 30 + 19 + 23 = 76

BIRTH/DAY # `-NUMBER = 76 / (DIVIDED by) (`-2) = 38 = RECIPROCAL = 83 = `-DIED within `-HIS 83rd YEAR of EXISTENCE!!!~'

BIRTH/YEAR = 19/23 = (19 + 23) = 42 = (7 X 6) = BIRTH/DAY # `-NUMBER!!!~'

DEATHDAY # `-NUMBER = 2/3/20/06 = 2 + 3 + 20 + 06 = 31

(76 (-) 31) = 45 / (DIVIDED by) ('-2) = 22.5 = ROUNDED UP = 2/3 = DEATH/DAY!!!~'

(76 (-) 31) = 45 / (DIVIDED by) ('-2) = 22.5 = "FLIP EVERY ('-2) OVER to a ('-7)" = 77.5 = (77 + 5) = ('-82) = AGE of DEATH for AMERICAN ACTOR AL LEWIS (THE MUNSTERS)!!!~'

BIRTH/DAY = 4/30 = (30 (-) 4) = 26 = DEATH/YEAR = (20 + 06) = 26

FRAGMENTED BIRTHDAY # '-NUMBER = 4 + 3 + 0 + 1 + 9 + 2 + 3 = 22

FRAGMENTED DEATHDAY # '-NUMBER = 2 + 3 + 2 + 0 + 0 + 6 = 13

FRAGMENTED DEATH/DAY # '-NUMBER = 13 = BIRTH/DAY # '-NUMBER = 76 = (7 + 6) = ('-13)!!!~'

(13 + 13) = 26 = DEATH/YEAR = (20 + 06) = ('-26)!!!~'

FRAGMENTED DEATH/DAY # '-NUMBER = 13 = RECIPROCAL = 31 = DEATH/DAY # '-NUMBER!!!~'

(22 + 13) = 35 = (5 X 7) = 57 YEARS '-ACTIVE from 1949 TO 2006!!!~'

(22 + 13) = (2 x 2) (1 x 3) = ('-43) = "SEE '-BELOW"!!!~'

DEATH/YEAR = 06 = RECIPROCAL = 60 = HEIGHT = 6' 0"!!!~'

WAS '-MARRIED to KAREN INGENTHRON from 1984 to 2006 = 22 YEARS = FRAGMENTED BIRTH/DAY # '-NUMBER!!!~'

WAS `-MARRIED to MARGE LEWIS from 1956 to 1977 = 21 YEARS!!!~'

WAS `-MARRIED for (`-43) YEARS = BIRTH/DAY = 4/30 = (4 + 30) = (`-34) = RECIPROCAL = (`-43)!!!~'

(`-43) (X TIMES) (`-2) = (`-86)!!!~'

FROM BIRTH-TO-DEATH there are 86 DAYS!!!~'

(365 (-) 86) = 279 = (27 x 9) = 243 = (`-2) (X TIMES) (`-43)!!!~'

(365 (-) 86) = 279 = (79 x 2) = 158 = RECIPROCAL = 851 = (8) (5 + 1) = (`-86)!!!~'

BIRTH/YEAR = 19/23 = (1 – 9) (2 x 3) = (`-86) = DAYS from BIRTH-TO-DEATH!!!~'

AMERICAN POLITICAL SATIRIST AND JOURNALIST PATRICK JAKE O'ROURKE died at the AGE of 74!!!~'

BIRTH/YEAR = 1947 = (1 – 9 – 4) (7) = 47 = RECIPROCAL = 74 = AGE of DEATH for AMERICAN POLITICAL SATIRIST AND JOURNALIST PATRICK JAKE O'ROURKE!!!~'

BIRTHDAY # `-NUMBER = 11/14/19/47 = 11 + 14 + 19 + 47 = 91

DEATHDAY # `-NUMBER = 2/15/20/22 = 2 + 15 + 20 + 22 = 59

(91 (-) 59) = 32 = -a PROPHETIC # `-NUMBER!!!~'

BIRTH/DAY = 11/14 = (11 + 14) = (`-25) = "FLIP EVERY (`-2) OVER to a (`-7) = (`-75) = DIED within HIS 75th YEAR of EXISTENCE!!!~'

DEATH/DAY = 2/15 = (25 x 1) = ('-25) = "FLIP EVERY ('-2) OVER to a ('-7) = ('-75) = DIED within HIS 75ᵗʰ YEAR of EXISTENCE!!!~'

BIRTH/YEAR = 47 = "FLIP EVERY ('-7) OVER to a ('-2)" = 42 = DEATH/YEAR = (20 + 22) = 42!!!~'

BIRTH/DAY = 11/14 = (11 x 14) = 154 = (54 x 1) = 54 = RECIPROCAL = 45 = (5 X 9) = DEATH/DAY # '-NUMBER!!!~'

FRAGMENTED BIRTHDAY # '-NUMBER = 1 + 1 + 1 + 4 + 1 + 9 + 4 + 7 = 28

FRAGMENTED BIRTH/DAY # '-NUMBER = 28 = (7 X 4) = AGE of DEATH for AMERICAN POLITICAL SATIRIST AND JOURNALIST PATRICK JAKE O'ROURKE!!!~'

FRAGMENTED DEATHDAY # '-NUMBER = 2 + 1 + 5 + 2 + 0 + 2 + 2 = 14

(28 + 14) = 42 = "FLIP EVERY ('-2) OVER to a ('-7)" = 47 = RECIPROCAL = 74 = AGE of DEATH for AMERICAN POLITICAL SATIRIST AND JOURNALIST PATRICK JAKE O'ROURKE!!!~'

(28 + 14) = 42 = DEATH/YEAR = (20 + 22) = 42

WAS '-MARRIED to TINA O'ROURKE from 1995 to 2022 = 27 YEARS!!!~'

(27 (-) 3) = 24 = RECIPROCAL = 42

WAS '-MARRIED to AMY LUMET from 1990 to 1993 = 3 YEARS!!!~' /|\ (90, 91,92,93) = 4

YEARS '-MARRIED = '-2(74)

FROM BIRTH-TO-DEATH there are 93 DAYS = (9 x 3) = 27 = YEARS `-MARRIED to TINA O'ROURKE!!!~'

(365 (-) 93) = 272 = (2 + 72) = 74 = AGE of DEATH for AMERICAN POLITICAL SATIRIST AND JOURNALIST PATRICK JAKE O'ROURKE!!!~'

BIRTH/YEAR = (`-47) = RECIPROCAL = (`-74) = AGE of DEATH for AMERICAN POLITICAL SATIRIST AND JOURNALIST PATRICK JAKE O'ROURKE!!!~'

MUSICAL ARTIST/ACTOR - MEAT LOAF - (MICHAEL LEE ADAY) was BORN in (47) = RECIPROCAL = (74) = AGE of DEATH!!!~' RAY FOSSE (AMERICAN BASEBALL PLAYER) was BORN in (47) & RECIPROCAL = (74) = AGE of DEATH!~' HIS `-BIRTHDAY # `-NUMBER = 4+4+19+47 = 74!~' This is a PATTERN in MY 11 BOOKS!!!~'

JEREMY DEAN GIAMBI BIRTH/YEAR = 74 = RECIPROCAL = 47 = AGE of DEATH for AMERICAN PROFESSIONAL BASEBALL PLAYER JEREMY DEAN GIAMBI!!!~' BIRTHDAY = 9+30+19+74 = 132 & DIED 132 DAYS from BIRTH-TO-DEATH!!!~' SAME for MEAT LOAF & RAY FOSSE BORN in 47 & DIED in 74 with FOSSE'S BIRTHDAY = 74!!!~'

AMERICAN POLITICAL SATIRIST AND JOURNALIST PATRICK JAKE O'ROURKE died at the AGE of (`-74); WHILE, being `-BORN in (`-47)!!!~' JUST LIKE MEAT LOAF & RAY FOSSE `-DIED at (`-74) RECIPROCAL while being `-BORN in (`-47)!!!~' JUST LIKE JEREMY DEAN GIAMBI was BORN in (`-74) AND DIED AT AGE (`-47)!!!~'

AMERICAN ACTRESS CAROLYN SUE JONES (THE ADDAMS FAMILY) died at the AGE of 53!!!~'

DEATH/DAY # '-NUMBER in '-REVERSE = (83 (-) 19 (-) 3 (-) 8) = 53 = AGE of DEATH for AMERICAN ACTRESS CAROLYN SUE JONES (THE ADDAMS FAMILY)!!!~'

BIRTH/YEAR = 19/30 = (1 – 9) (3 + 0) = 8/3 = DEATH/DAY & DEATH/YEAR ('-83)!!!~'

BIRTHDAY # '-NUMBER = 4/28/19/30 = 4 + 28 + 19 + 30 = 81

DEATHDAY # '-NUMBER = 8/3/19/83 = 8 + 3 + 19 + 83 = 113

DEATH/DAY # '-NUMBER = 113 = "FLIP EVERY ('-3) OVER to an ('-8)" = 118 = RECIPROCAL = 811 = (8) (1 x 1) = 81 = BIRTH/DAY # '-NUMBER!!!~'

(113 (-) 81) = 32 = -a PROPHETIC # '-NUMBER = FRAGMENTED DEATH/DAY # '-NUMBER = ('-32) = BIRTH/DAY = 4/28 = (4 + 28) = ('-32)!!!~'

DEATH/DAY = 8/3 = DEATH/YEAR = ('-83)!!!~'

(81/113) = (8 x 1) (1 x 1 x 3) = 8/3 = DEATH/DAY!!!~'

(81/113) = (8 – 3) (1 + 1 + 1) = 53 = AGE of DEATH for AMERICAN ACTRESS CAROLYN SUE JONES (THE ADDAMS FAMILY)!!!~'

BIRTH/DAY = 4/28 = (28 (-) 4) = 24

DEATH/DAY = 8/3 = (8 x 3) = 24

FRAGMENTED BIRTHDAY # '-NUMBER = 4 + 2 + 8 + 1 + 9 + 3 + 0 = 27

FRAGMENTED DEATHDAY # `-NUMBER = 8 + 3 + 1 + 9 + 8 + 3 = 32

FRAGMENTED DEATH/DAY # `-NUMBER = 32 = -a PROPHETIC # `-NUMBER!!!~'

(27 + 32) = 59 (X TIMES) (`-2) = 118 = "FLIP EVERY (`-8) OVER to a (`-3)" = 113 = DEATH/DAY # `-NUMBER!!!~'

YEARS ACTIVE were FROM 1952 to 1983 = 31 YEARS = "FLIP EVERY (`-3) OVER to an (`-8)" = 81 = BIRTH/DAY # `-NUMBER!!!~'

FROM BIRTH-TO-DEATH there are 97 DAYS = (9 x 7) = 63 = "FLIP EVERY (`-3) OVER to an (`-8)" = (`-68)!!!~'

(365 (-) 97) = 268 = (26 (-) 8) = 18 = RECIPROCAL = 81 = BIRTH/DAY # `-NUMBER!!!~'

WAS `-BORN in the `-MONTH of (`-4); AND, `-DIED in the `-MONTH of (`-8) = 4/8 = (4 x 8) = 32 = FRAGMENTED DEATH/DAY # `-NUMBER = BIRTH/DAY = 4/28 = (4 + 28) = (`-32)!!!~'

WAS `-MARRIED to PETER BAILEY-BRITTON from 19(82) to 19(83) = (`-1) YEAR!!!~'

WAS `-MARRIED to HERBERT GREENE from 19(68) to 19(77) = (`-9) YEARS!!!~'

BIRTH/YEAR = 19/30 = (19 + 30) = 49 = (7 X 7) = (`-77)!!!~'

DEATH/YEAR = 19/83 = (83 (-) 19) = (`-64)!!!~'

WAS `-MARRIED to AARON SPELLING from 19(53) to 19(64) = (`-11) YEARS!!!~'

WAS `-FIRST `-MARRIED in (`-53); and, `-DIED at the AGE (`-53) of DEATH for AMERICAN ACTRESS CAROLYN SUE JONES (THE ADDAMS FAMILY)!!!~'

AMERICAN ACTOR THEODORE CRAWFORD CASSIDY (LURCH) (THE ADDAMS FAMILY) died at the AGE of 46!!!~'

BIRTH/YEAR = 32 = RECIPROCAL = 23 (X TIMES) (`-2) = (`-46) = AGE of DEATH for AMERICAN ACTOR THEODORE CRAWFORD CASSIDY (LURCH) (THE ADDAMS FAMILY)!!!~'

BIRTHDAY # `-NUMBER = 7/31/19/32 = 7 + 31 + 19 + 32 = 89

BIRTHDAY # `-NUMBER = 89 = RECIPROCAL = 98 = DEATH/YEAR = (19 + 79) = 98

DEATHDAY # `-NUMBER = 1/16/19/79 = 1 + 16 + 19 + 79 = 115

(115 (-) 89) = 26 = DEATH/DAY = 1/16 = (1 + 1) (6) = 26 = FRAGMENTED BIRTH/DAY # `-NUMBER = 26!!!~'

(115 + 89) = 204 = (24 + 0) = 24 = BIRTH/DAY = 7/31 = (31 (-) 7) = 24

BIRTH/DAY = 7/31 = (7) (3 + 1) = 74 = RECIPROCAL = 47 = DIED within HIS (`-47th) YEAR of EXISTENCE!!!~'

BIRTH/DAY = 7/31 = "FLIP EVERY (`-3) OVER to an (`-8)" = 7/81 = (7) (8 + 1) = 79 = DEATH/YEAR!!!~'

DEATH/DAY = 1/16 = HALF RECIPROCAL = 1/61 = (1 + 61) = 62 / (DIVIDED by) (`-2) = 31 = DAY of `-BIRTH!!!~'

FRAGMENTED BIRTHDAY # `-NUMBER = 7 + 3 + 1 + 1 + 9 +3 + 2 = 26

FRAGMENTED DEATHDAY # `-NUMBER = 1 + 1 + 6 + 1 + 9 +7 + 9 = 34

(26 + 34) = 60 = DEATH/YEAR = (19 (-) 79) = 60 = DEATH/DAY = 1/16 = RECIPROCAL = 61/1 = (61 (-) 1) = (`-60)!!!~'

WAS `-BORN in the `-MONTH of (`-7); AND, `-DIED in the `-MONTH of (`-1) = 7/1 = RECIPROCAL = 1/7!!!~'

(71 (-) 17) = (`-54) = (9 X 6) = 9' 6" = HEIGHT!!!~'

DEATH/MONTH = JANUARY = 31 DAYS!!!~'

(31 (-) 16) – (DAY of DEATH) = 15 = RECIPROCAL = 51 = BIRTH/ YEAR = (19 + 32) = 51!!!~'

HEIGHT = 6' 9" = (6 + 9) = 15 = RECIPROCAL = 51 = BIRTH/ YEAR = (19 + 32) = 51 = DEATH/DAY # `-NUMBER = 115 = RECIPROCAL = 511 = (5) (1 x 1) = (`-51)!!!~'

WAS `-MARRIED to MARGARET HELEN JESSE from 1956 to 1975 = 19 YEARS = (1 + 9) = 10 = (4 + 6) = 46 = AGE of DEATH for AMERICAN ACTOR THEODORE CRAWFORD CASSIDY (LURCH) (THE ADDAMS FAMILY)!!!~'

YEARS ACTIVE were from 1959 TO 1979 = 20 YEARS = (5 X 4) = 54 = (6 X 9) = HEIGHT = 6' 9"!!!~'

FROM BIRTH-TO-DEATH there are 196 DAYS = (1 + 6) (9) = 79 = DEATH/YEAR!!!~'

FROM BIRTH-TO-DEATH there are 196 DAYS = RECIPROCAL = 691 = (69 x 1) = 69 = 6' 9" = HEIGHT!!!~'

(365 (-) 196 = 169 = (1 + 6) (9) = 79 = DEATH/YEAR!!!~'

BIRTH/YEAR = 19/32 = (9) (3 + 2 − 1) = 94 = RECIPROCAL = 49 = "FLIP EVERY ('-9) OVER to a ('-6)" = 46 = AGE of DEATH for AMERICAN ACTOR THEODORE CRAWFORD CASSIDY (LURCH) (THE ADDAMS FAMILY)!!!~'

AMERICAN ACTOR KENNETH PATRICK WEATHERWAX (THE ADDAMS FAMILY) died at the AGE of 59!!!~'

BIRTH/DAY # '-NUMBER = 112 / (DIVIDED by) ('-2) = ('-56) = "FLIP EVERY ('-6) OVER to a ('-9)" = ('-59) = AGE of DEATH for AMERICAN ACTOR KENNETH PATRICK WEATHERWAX (THE ADDAMS FAMILY)!!!~'

BIRTHDAY # '-NUMBER = 9/29/19/55 = 9 + 29 + 19 + 55 = 112

DEATHDAY # '-NUMBER = 12/7/20/14 = 12 + 7 + 20 + 14 = 53

(112 (-) 53) = 59 = AGE of DEATH for AMERICAN ACTOR KENNETH PATRICK WEATHERWAX (THE ADDAMS FAMILY)!!!~'

FRAGMENTED BIRTHDAY # '-NUMBER = 9 + 2 + 9 + 1 + 9 + 5 + 5 = 40

FRAGMENTED DEATHDAY # '-NUMBER = 1 + 2 + 7 + 2 + 0 + 1 + 4 = 17

$(40/17) = (4 + 0)(1 \times 7) = 47 = \text{RECIPROCAL} = 74 = \text{BIRTH/YEAR}$
$= (19 + 55) = 74$

$(40 + 17) = 57 = (5 \times 7) = 35 = \text{RECIPROCAL} = 53 = \text{DEATH/DAY}$
`-NUMBER!!!~'

$(40 \, (\text{-}) \, 17) = (\text{`-}23) = \text{-a PROPHETIC \#} \text{ `-NUMBER!!!~'}$

FROM BIRTH-TO-DEATH there are 69 DAYS $= (6 \times 9) = 54 =$
RECIPROCAL $= 45 = (5 \times 9) = $ AGE of DEATH for AMERICAN
ACTOR KENNETH PATRICK WEATHERWAX (THE ADDAMS
FAMILY)!!!~'

$(365 \, (\text{-}) \, 69) = 296 = (2 \times 96) = 192 = (1 \times 92) = 92 = \text{RECIPROCAL}$
$= 29 = \text{DAY of `-BIRTH!!!~'}$

WAS `-BORN in the `-MONTH of (`-9); AND, `-DIED in the
`-MONTH of (`-12) $= 9/12 = (92 \times 1) = 92 = $ RECIPROCAL $= 29 =$
DAY of `-BIRTH!!!~'

BIRTH/YEAR $= 19/55 = (1 + 9 + 5)(5) = (15)(5) = (1 + 5)(5) = 65 =$
RECIPROCAL $= 56 = $ "FLIP EVERY (`-6) OVER to a (`-9)" $= (\text{`-}59)$
$= $ AGE of DEATH for AMERICAN ACTOR KENNETH PATRICK
WEATHERWAX (THE ADDAMS FAMILY)!!!~'

AMERICAN ACTRESS BLOSSOM ROCK (EDITH MARIE
BLOSSOM MACDONALD) (THE ADDAMS FAMILY) died at
the AGE of 82!!!~'

BIRTH/DAY $= 8/21 = (82 \times 1) = 82 = $ AGE of DEATH for
AMERICAN ACTRESS BLOSSOM ROCK (EDITH MARIE
BLOSSOM MACDONALD) (THE ADDAMS FAMILY)!!!~'

BIRTH/YEAR = 18/95 = (18 + 95) = 113 = "FLIP EVERY ('-3) OVER to an ('-8)" = 118 = RECIPROCAL = 811 = (8) (1 + 1) = 82 = AGE of DEATH for AMERICAN ACTRESS BLOSSOM ROCK (EDITH MARIE BLOSSOM MACDONALD) (THE ADDAMS FAMILY)!!!~'

BIRTHDAY # '-NUMBER = 8/21/18/95 = 8 + 21 + 18 + 95 = 142

BIRTH/DAY # '-NUMBER = 142 = (1 + 2) (4) = 34 = FRAGMENTED BIRTH/DAY # '-NUMBER!!!~'

DEATHDAY # '-NUMBER = 1/14/19/78 = 1 + 14 + 19 + 78 = 112

(142 + 112) = 254 = (2 x 54) = 108 = (10 + 8) = 18 = RECIPROCAL = 81 = WAS '-BORN in the '-MONTH of ('-8); AND, '-DIED in the '-MONTH of ('-1)!!!~'

DEATH/YEAR = 19/78 = (1 – 9) (7 – 8) = ('-81)!!!~'

BIRTH/DAY = 8/21 = (21 (-) 8) = 13 = RECIPROCAL = 31 = "FLIP EVERY ('-3) OVER to an ('-8)" = ('-81)!!!~'

DEATH/DAY = 1/14 = RECIPROCAL = 41/1 = (4 – 1) (1) = 31 = "FLIP EVERY ('-3) OVER to an ('-8)" = ('-81)!!!~'

BIRTH/DAY # '-NUMBER = 142 = (1 x 42) = 42 = DEATH/DAY = 1/14 = RECIPROCAL = 41/1 = (41 + 1) = ('-42)!!!~'

DAY of '-DEATH = 14th = RECIPROCAL = 41 (X TIMES) ('-2) = 82 = AGE of DEATH for AMERICAN ACTRESS BLOSSOM ROCK (EDITH MARIE BLOSSOM MACDONALD) (THE ADDAMS FAMILY)!!!~'

BIRTH/DAY = 8/21 = (8 + 1) (2) = 92 = "FLIP EVERY ('-2) OVER to a ('-7)" = 97 = DEATH/YEAR = (19 + 78) = ('-97)!!!~'

FRAGMENTED BIRTHDAY # `-NUMBER = 8 + 2 + 1 + 1 + 8 + 9 + 5 = 34

FRAGMENTED DEATHDAY # `-NUMBER = 1 + 1 + 4 + 1 + 9 + 7 + 8 = 31

(34 + 31) = 65 = RECIPROCAL = 56 = "SEE BELOW" for TIME of BIRTH/DAY to DEATH/DAY!!!~'

DEATH/DAY # `-NUMBER = 112 / (DIVIDED by) (`-2) = (`-56)!!!~'

WAS `-MARRIED to CLARENCE ROCK from 1926 to 1960 = 34 YEARS = FRAGMENTED BIRTH/DAY # `-NUMBER = (`-34)!!!~'

(`-34) = RECIPROCAL = (`-43)

YEARS `-ACTIVE from 19(23) TO 19(66) = (`-43) = RECIPROCAL = (`-34) = YEARS `-MARRIED = FRAGMENTED BIRTH/DAY # `-NUMBER!!!~'

FROM BIRTH-TO-DEATH there are 146 DAYS = (1 + 4) (6) = (`-56) = "FLIP EVERY (`-6) OVER to a (`-9)" = 59 = RECIPROCAL = 95 = BIRTH/YEAR!!!~'

DEATH/YEAR = (`-78) = (7 x 8) = (`-56)!!!~'

(365 (-) 146) = 219 = RECIPROCAL = 912 = (9 – 1) (2) = 82 = AGE of DEATH for AMERICAN ACTRESS BLOSSOM ROCK (EDITH MARIE BLOSSOM MACDONALD) (THE ADDAMS FAMILY)!!!~'

BIRTH/YEAR = (`-95) = RECIPROCAL = (`-59) = DEATH/YEAR = (19 – 78) = (`-59)!!!~'

ITALIAN-BORN ACTOR FELIX ANTHONY SILLA (THE ADDAMS FAMILY) died at the AGE of 84!!!~'

BIRTH/YEAR = 19/37 = (1 – 9) (3 – 7) = 84 = AGE of DEATH for ITALIAN-BORN ACTOR FELIX ANTHONY SILLA (THE ADDAMS FAMILY)!!!~'

BIRTHDAY # '-NUMBER = 1/11/19/37 = 1 + 11 + 19 + 37 = 68

BIRTH/DAY # '-NUMBER = 68 = (6 x 8) = 48 = RECIPROCAL = 84 = AGE of DEATH for ITALIAN-BORN ACTOR FELIX ANTHONY SILLA (THE ADDAMS FAMILY)!!!~'

DEATHDAY # '-NUMBER = 4/16/20/21 = 4 + 16 + 20 + 21 = 61

(68 + 61) = 129 = (1 + 2) (9) = 39 = FRAG BIRTH/DEATH DAYS '-ADDED '-UP '-TOGETHER!!!~'

BIRTH/YEAR = 37 = "FLIP EVERY ('-7) OVER to a ('-2)" = 32 = -a PROPHETIC # '-NUMBER = (8 X 4) = AGE of DEATH for ITALIAN-BORN ACTOR FELIX ANTHONY SILLA (THE ADDAMS FAMILY)!!!~'

('-23) = RECIPROCAL = ('-32)

DEATH/DAY = 4/16 = (46 x 1) = 46 / (DIVIDED by) ('-2) = ('-23) = -a PROPHETIC # '-NUMBER = FRAGMENTED BIRTH/DAY # '-NUMBER ('-23)!!!~'

FRAGMENTED BIRTHDAY # '-NUMBER = 1 + 1 + 1 + 1 + 9 + 3 + 7 = 23

FRAGMENTED BIRTH/DAY # '-NUMBER = 23 = RECIPROCAL = 32 = (8 X 4) = AGE of DEATH for ITALIAN-BORN ACTOR FELIX ANTHONY SILLA (THE ADDAMS FAMILY)!!!~'

FRAGMENTED DEATHDAY # `-NUMBER = 4 + 1 + 6 + 2 + 0 + 2 + 1 = 16

FRAGMENTED DEATH/DAY # `-NUMBER = 16 = RECIPROCAL = 61 = DEATH/DAY # `-NUMBER!!!~'

FRAGMENTED DEATH/DAY # `-NUMBER = 16 = DAY of `-DEATH = (`-16ᵗʰ)!!!~'

(23 + 16) = 39 = "SEE `-ABOVE & `-BELOW" = "FLIP EVERY (`-3) OVER to an (`-8)"; "FLIP EVERY (`-9) OVER to a (`-6)" = 86 = RECIPROCAL = 68 = BIRTH/DAY # `-NUMBER!!!~'

HEIGHT = 3' 11" = BIRTH/DAY = 1/11 = 3(1's) 1(937) = (3/11)!!!~'

(`-937) = (9 + 37) = 46 = DEATH/DAY = 4/16 = (46 x 1) = (`-46)!!!~'

DEATH/DAY = 4/16 = (4 + 1) (6) = (`-56)!!!~'

WAS `-MARRIED to EVELYN SUE SILLA from 19(65) to 2021 = (`-56) YEARS!!!~'

BIRTH/YEAR = 19/37 = (19 + 37) = (`-56) = YEARS `-MARRIED!!!~'

WAS `-MARRIED in (`-65) = RECIPROCAL = (`-56) = MARRIAGE `-LASTED!!!~'

DEATH/DAY = 4/16 = RECIPROCAL = 61/4 = (61 + 4) = (`-65)!!!~'

BECAME `-ACTIVE in (`-64) = (6 x 4) = 24 = RECIPROCAL = 42 (X TIMES) (`-2) = 84 = AGE of DEATH for ITALIAN-BORN ACTOR FELIX ANTHONY SILLA (THE ADDAMS FAMILY)!!!~'

YEARS `-ACTIVE were from 19(64) to (2019) = (`-55) YEARS!!!~'

WAS `-BORN in the `-MONTH of (`-1); AND, `-DIED in the `-MONTH of (`-4) = 1/4 = RECIPROCAL = 4/1!!!~'

(14 + 41) = (`-55)!!!~'

WAS NO LONGER `-ACTIVE in (20/19) = (20 + 19) = (`-39)!!!~'

FROM BIRTH-TO-DEATH there are 95 DAYS = BIRTH/YEAR = 19/37 = (9) (7 – 3 + 1) = (`-95)!!!-'

(365 (-) 95) = 270 = (27 + 0) = 27 = (3 X 9) = FRAG BIRTH/DEATH DAYS `-ADDED `-UP `-TOGETHER!!!~'

`-FOCUS on the `-VISUAL `-IMAGE of AN `-ACTUAL `-EMBRYO!!!~' THIS `-CREATED from `-ONE `-CELL (ZYGOTE); AND, THEN; the `-EVENTUALITY of `-YOU!!!~'

`-GOD USES `-ALL of `-US, for WHEN, the `-TIME; is `-RIGHT!!!~'

AMERICAN ACTOR JOHN CARROLL O'CONNOR (ALL IN THE FAMILY) died at the AGE of 76!!!~'

BIRTH/YEAR = 24 = RECIPROCAL = 42 = (7 X 6) = AGE of DEATH for AMERICAN ACTOR JOHN CARROLL O'CONNOR (ALL IN THE FAMILY)!!!~'

BIRTHDAY # `-NUMBER = 8/2/19/24 = 8 + 2 + 19 + 24 = 53

DEATHDAY # `-NUMBER = 6/21/20/01 = 6 + 21 + 20 + 01 = 48

(53 + 48) = 101 = (10 x 1) = 10 = BIRTH/DAY = 8/2 = (8 + 2) = 10

DEATH/DAY = 6/21 = "FLIP EVERY (`-2) OVER to a (`-7)" = 6/71 = (67 x 1) = 67 = RECIPROCAL = 76 = AGE of DEATH for AMERICAN ACTOR JOHN CARROLL O'CONNOR (ALL IN THE FAMILY)!!!~'

DAY of `-DEATH = 21 = DEATH/YEAR = (20 + 01) = 21

(21 + 21) = 42 = (7 X 6) = AGE of DEATH for AMERICAN ACTOR JOHN CARROLL O'CONNOR (ALL IN THE FAMILY)!!!~'

FRAGMENTED BIRTHDAY # `-NUMBER = 8 + 2 + 1 + 9 + 2 + 4 = 26

FRAGMENTED BIRTH/DAY # `-NUMBER = 26 = "FLIP EVERY (`-2) OVER to a (`-7) = 76 = AGE of DEATH for AMERICAN ACTOR JOHN CARROLL O'CONNOR (ALL IN THE FAMILY)!!!~'

FRAGMENTED DEATHDAY # `-NUMBER = 6 + 2 + 1 + 2 + 0 + 0 + 1 = 12

(26 + 12) = 38 = (3 x 8) = 24 = RECIPROCAL = 42 = (7 X 6) = AGE of DEATH for AMERICAN ACTOR JOHN CARROLL O'CONNOR (ALL IN THE FAMILY)!!!~'

(26 (-) 12) = 14 = (8 + 6) = WAS `-BORN in the `-MONTH of (`-8); AND, `-DIED in the `-MONTH of (`-6) = (8/6)!!!~'

(8 x 6) = 48 = DEATH/DAY # `-NUMBER!!!~'

WAS `-MARRIED to NANCY FIELDS O'CONNOR from 19(51) TO 2001 = 50 YEARS!!!~'

YEARS `-ACTIVE were from 19(51) to 2000 = 49 YEARS = (7 X 7)
= DIED within `-HIS (`-77ᵗʰ) YEAR of `-EXISTENCE!!!~'

GOT `-MARRIED & BECAME `-ACTIVE in (`-51) = HEIGHT =
5' 11"!!!~'

(19/51) = (19 – 51) = 32 = RECIPROCAL = 23 = -a PROPHETIC #
`-NUMBER!!!~'

FROM BIRTH-TO-DEATH there are 42 DAYS = (7 X 6) = AGE of
DEATH for AMERICAN ACTOR JOHN CARROLL O'CONNOR
(ALL IN THE FAMILY)!!!~'

(365 (-) 42) = 323 = Reciprocal/Sequencing/Numerology-RSN = (3
+ 2) (3) = 53 = BIRTH/DAY # `-NUMBER!!!~'

BIRTH/YEAR = 19/24 = (9) (1 + 2 + 4) = 97 = RECIPROCAL = 79
= "FLIP EVERY (`-9) OVER to a (`-6)" = 76 = AGE of DEATH for
AMERICAN ACTOR JOHN CARROLL O'CONNOR (ALL IN
THE FAMILY)!!!~'

BIRTH/MONTH = AUGUST = 31 DAYS!!!~'

(31 (-) 2) – (DAY of BIRTH) = 29 = "FLIP EVERY (`-2) OVER to a
(`-7)"; "FLIP EVERY (`-9) OVER to a (`-6)" = 76 = AGE of DEATH
for AMERICAN ACTOR JOHN CARROLL O'CONNOR (ALL
IN THE FAMILY)!!!~'

AMERICAN ACTRESS JEAN STAPLETON (ALL IN THE
FAMILY) died at the -AGE of 90!!!~'

BIRTH/DAY = 1/19 = RECIPROCAL = 91/1 = (91 (-) 1) = 90 = AGE of DEATH for AMERICAN ACTRESS JEAN STAPLETON (ALL IN THE FAMILY)!!!~'

'-AGE of '-DEATH = 90 / (DIVIDED by) ('-2) = 45 = DEATH/DAY = 5/31 = (5) (3 + 1) = 54 = RECIPROCAL = ('-45)!!!~'

BIRTHDAY # '-NUMBER = 1/19/19/23 = 1 + 19 + 19 + 23 = 62

BIRTH/DAY # '-NUMBER = 62 = BIRTH/DAY = 1/19 = "FLIP EVERY ('-9) OVER to a ('-6)" = 1/16 = (1 + 1) (6) = 26 = RECIPROCAL = ('-62)!!!~'

DEATHDAY # '-NUMBER = 5/31/20/13 = 5 + 31 + 20 + 13 = 69

(69 + 62) = 131 = (1 + 31) = 32 = RECIPROCAL = 23 = BIRTH/YEAR!!!~'

DEATH/DAY = 5/31 = (5) (3 + 1) = 54 = RECIPROCAL = 45 (X TIMES) ('-2) = 90 = AGE of DEATH for AMERICAN ACTRESS JEAN STAPLETON (ALL IN THE FAMILY)!!!~'

DEATH/DAY # '-NUMBER = 69 = (6 x 9) = 54 = RECIPROCAL = 45 (X TIMES) ('-2) = 90 = AGE of DEATH for AMERICAN ACTRESS JEAN STAPLETON (ALL IN THE FAMILY)!!!~'

FRAGMENTED BIRTHDAY # '-NUMBER = 1 + 1 + 9 + 1 + 9 + 2 + 3 = 26

FRAGMENTED BIRTH/DAY # '-NUMBER = 26 = WAS '-MARRIED for ('-26) YEARS = RECIPROCAL = 62 = BIRTH/DAY # '-NUMBER!!!~'

DEATH/DAY = 5/31 = (31 (-) 5) = ('-26) = "SEE '-ABOVE & '-BELOW"!!!~'

FRAGMENTED DEATHDAY # `-NUMBER = 5 + 3 + 1 + 2 + 0 + 1 + 3 = 15

(26 /|\ 15) = (2 – 6) (1 x 5) = 45 (X TIMES) (`-2) = 90 = AGE of DEATH for AMERICAN ACTRESS JEAN STAPLETON (ALL IN THE FAMILY)!!!~'

(26 + 15) = 41 = YEARS `-ACTIVE were from 19(41) TO (2001) = 60 YEARS = "FLIP EVERY (`-6) OVER to a (`-9)" = 90 = AGE of DEATH for AMERICAN ACTRESS JEAN STAPLETON (ALL IN THE FAMILY)!!!~'

STARTED BEING `-ACTIVE in (`-41)!!!~'

HEIGHT = 5' 8' = DEATH/DAY = 5/31 = (53 x 1) = 53 = "FLIP EVERY (`-3) OVER to an (`-8)" = (`-58)!!!~'

WAS `-MARRIED to WILLIAM H. PUTCH from 19(57) TO 19(83) = 26 = FRAGMENTED BIRTH/DAY # `-NUMBER = RECIPROCAL = 62 = BIRTH/DAY # `-NUMBER!!!~'

(1957) = (19 + 57) = 76 = "FLIP EVERY (`-7) OVER to a (`-2) = (`-26)!!!~'

FROM BIRTH-TO-DEATH = 132 = (13 x 2) = (`-26)!!!~'

WAS `-MARRIED in (`-57) = (5 x 7) = (`-35) = RECIPROCAL = (`-53) = "SEE `-ABOVE & `-BELOW"!!!~'

FROM BIRTH-TO-DEATH there are 132 DAYS = (1 x 32) = 32 = -a PROPHETIC # `-NUMBER = RECIPROCAL = 23 = BIRTH/YEAR!!!~'

(365 (-) 132) = 233 = (2 + 3) (3) = 53 = DEATH/DAY = 5/31 = (53 x 1) = (`-53)!!!~'

(ALL in the FAMILY) (RE-READ; the `-TWO, `-TOGETHER; including, the BIRTH-TO-DEATHS)!!!~'

JEAN STAPLETON (`-132) /|\ JOHN CARROLL O'CONNOR (`-323)!!!~'

NORWEGIAN-AMERICAN PLAYER AND COACH KNUTE KENNETH ROCKNE died at the AGE of 43!!!~

BIRTH/DAY = 3/4 = RECIPROCAL = 4/3 = AGE of DEATH for NORWEGIAN-AMERICAN PLAYER AND COACH KNUTE KENNETH ROCKNE!!!~'

DEATH/DAY = 3/31 = (3) (3 + 1) = 34 = RECIPROCAL = 43 = AGE of DEATH for NORWEGIAN-AMERICAN PLAYER AND COACH KNUTE KENNETH ROCKNE!!!~'

BIRTHDAY # `-NUMBER = 3/4/18/88 = 3 + 4 + 18 + 88 = 113

BIRTH/DAY # `-NUMBER = 113 = RECIPROCAL = 311 = (31 x 1) = 31 = DEATH/YEAR!!!~'

DAY of `-DEATH = (`-31) = DEATH/YEAR!!!~'

DEATHDAY # `=NUMBER = 3/31/19/31 = 3 + 31 + 19 + 31 = 84

DEATH/DAY # = 84 = "FLIP EVERY (`-8) OVER to a (`-3)" = 34 = RECIPROCAL = 43 = AGE of DEATH for NORWEGIAN-AMERICAN PLAYER AND COACH KNUTE KENNETH ROCKNE!!!~'

(113 + 84) = 197 = (19 x 7) = 133 = (1 + 3) (3) = 43 = AGE of DEATH for NORWEGIAN-AMERICAN PLAYER AND COACH KNUTE KENNETH ROCKNE!!!~'

DAY of `-BIRTH = (`-4) /|\ DAY of `-DEATH = (`-31) /|\ (4/31) = (43 x 1) = 43 = AGE of DEATH for NORWEGIAN-AMERICAN PLAYER AND COACH KNUTE KENNETH ROCKNE!!!~'

FRAGMENTED BIRTHDAY # `-NUMBER = 3 + 4 + 1 + 8 + 8 + 8 = 32

FRAGMENTED BIRTHDAY # `-NUMBER = 32 = -a PROPHETIC # `-NUMBER!!!~'

FRAGMENTED DEATHDAY # `-NUMBER = 3 + 3 + 1 + 1 + 9 + 3 + 1 = 21

(32 + 21) = 53 = "SEE `-BELOW"!!!~'

WAS `-MARRIED to BONNIE GWENDOLINE SKILES from 1914 TO 1931 = 17 YEARS = 17 (X TIMES) (`-2) = 34 = RECIPROCAL = 43 = AGE of DEATH for NORWEGIAN-AMERICAN PLAYER AND COACH KNUTE KENNETH ROCKNE!!!~'

FROM BIRTH-TO-DEATH there are 27 DAYS!!!~'

(365 (-) 27) = 338 = RECIPROCAL = 833 = (8 – 3) (3) = 53 = "SEE `-ABOVE"!!!~'

BIRTH/DAY = 34 = DEATH/DAY = 3/31 = (3 + 31) = 34!!!~'

AMERICAN FOOTBALL COACH VINCENT THOMAS LOMBARDI died at the AGE of 57!!!~'

BIRTHDAY # `-NUMBER = 6/11/19/13 = 6 + 11 + 19 + 13 = 49

DEATHDAY # `-NUMBER = 9/3/19/70 = 9 + 3 + 19 + 70 = 101

(101 (-) 49) = 52 = "FLIP EVERY (`-2) OVER to a (`-7)" = 57 = AGE of DEATH for AMERICAN FOOTBALL COACH VINCENT THOMAS LOMBARDI!!!~'

DEATH/DAY# `-NUMBER in `-REVERSE = (70 (-) 19 (-) 3 (-) 9) = 39 = BIRTH/YEAR = 19/13 = (1 x 9) (1 x 3) = 93 = RECIPROCAL = 39

FRAGMENTED BIRTHDAY # `-NUMBER = 6 + 1 + 1 + 1 + 9 + 1 + 3 = 22

FRAGMENTED DEATHDAY # `-NUMBER = 9 + 3 + 1 + 9 + 7 + 0 = 29

(22 + 29) = 51 = DEATH/YEAR = (19 – 70) = 51

(22 /|\ 29) = HALF RECIPROCAL = (22 /|\ 92) = (22 + 92) = 114 / (DIVIDED by) (`-2) = 57 = AGE of DEATH for AMERICAN FOOTBALL COACH VINCENT THOMAS LOMBARDI!!!~'

(92 (-) 22) = 70 = DEATH/YEAR!!!~'

FROM BIRTH-TO-DEATH there are 84 DAYS = (8 x 4) = 32 = -a PROPHETIC # `-NUMBER!!!~'

(365 (-) 84) = 281 = (81 x 2) = 162 = (1 – 6) (2) = 52 = "FLIP EVERY (`-2) OVER to a (`-7)" = 57 = AGE of DEATH for AMERICAN FOOTBALL COACH VINCENT THOMAS LOMBARDI!!!~'

BIRTH/YEAR = 19/13 = (1 x 9) (1 x 3) = 93 = DEATH/DAY!!!~'

AMERICAN FOOTBALL COACH BILL WALSH (WILLIAM ERNEST WALSH) died at the AGE of 75!!!~'

BIRTH/YEAR = 19/31 = (19 − 31) = 12 = (7 + 5) = AGE of DEATH for AMERICAN FOOTBALL COACH BILL WALSH!!!~'

BIRTHDAY # '-NUMBER = 11/30/19/31 = 11 + 30 + 19 + 31 = 91

DEATHDAY # '-NUMBER = 7/30/20/07 = 7 + 30 + 20 + 07 = 64

(91 + 64) = 155 = (15 x 5) = 75 = AGE of DEATH for AMERICAN FOOTBALL COACH BILL WALSH!!!~'

DEATH/DAY # '-NUMBER = 64 = 2 X 32 = Reciprocal/Sequencing/Numerology-RSN!!!~'

DEATH/DAY = 7/30 = (7 − 30) = ('-23) = -a PROPHETIC # '-NUMBER = ('-123) = DAYS from BIRTH-TO-DEATH!!!~'

DAY of '-BIRTH = 30 = DAY of '-DEATH = 30

FRAGMENTED BIRTHDAY # '-NUMBER = 1 + 1 + 3 + 0 + 1 + 9 + 3 + 1 = 19

FRAGMENTED DEATHDAY # '-NUMBER = 7 + 3 + 0 + 2 + 0 + 0 + 7 = 19

FRAGMENTED BIRTH/DAY # '-NUMBER = FRAGMENTED DEATH/DAY # '-NUMBER!!!~'

WAS '-MARRIED to GERI WALSH in ('-1954) = (19 − 54) = 35 = (7 X 5) = AGE of DEATH for AMERICAN FOOTBALL COACH BILL WALSH!!!~'

FROM BIRTH-TO-DEATH there are 123 DAYS = (1 x 23) = 23 = -a PROPHETIC # '-NUMBER!!!~'

(365 (-) 123) = 242 = Reciprocal/Sequencing/Numerology-RSN = (2 x 42) = 84 = (8 x 4) = (`-32) = RECIPROCAL = (`-23)!!!~'

BIRTH/DAY = 11/30 = (11 – 30) = 19 = RECIPROCAL = BIRTH/ DAY # `-NUMBER = 91 = RECIPROCAL = 19 = FRAGMENTED BIRTH/DAY # `-NUMBER = 19 = FRAGMENTED DEATH/DAY # `-NUMBER = 19!!!~'

BIRTH/YEAR = 19/31 = (1 x 9) (3 x 1) = 93 = DEATH/YEAR = (20 + 07) = 27 = (9 X 3)!!!~'

AMERICAN FOOTBALL PLAYER DWIGHT EDWARD CLARK died at the AGE of 61!!!~'

WAS `-BORN in the `-MONTH of (`-1); AND, `-DIED in the `-MONTH of (`-6) = 1/6 = RECIPROCAL = 6/1 = AGE of DEATH for AMERICAN FOOTBALL PLAYER DWIGHT EDWARD CLARK!!!~'

BIRTH/YEAR = 19/57 = (19 – 57) = 38 = DEATH/YEAR = (20 + 18) = 38

BIRTH/DAY = 1/8 (+) DEATH/DAY = 6/4 /|\ (1 + 8 + 6 + 4) = 19 (X TIMES) (`-2) = 38

(38 + 38) = 76 = BIRTH/YEAR = (19 + 57) = 76!!!~'

BIRTHDAY # `-NUMBER = 1/8/19/57 = 1 + 8 + 19 + 57 = 85

DEATHDAY # `-NUMBER = 6/4/20/18 = 6 + 4 + 20 + 18 = 48

(85 + 48) = 133 = (1) (3 + 3) = 16 = RECIPROCAL = 61 = AGE of DEATH for AMERICAN FOOTBALL PLAYER DWIGHT EDWARD CLARK!!!~'

BIRTH/DAY # '-NUMBER in '-REVERSE = (57 (-) 19 (-) 8 (-) 1) = 29 = DEATH/YEAR = 20/18 = (2 + 0) (1 + 8) = 29

(29 + 29) = 58 = RECIPROCAL = 85 = BIRTH/DAY # '-NUMBER!!!~'

FRAGMENTED BIRTHDAY # '-NUMBER = 1 + 8 + 1 + 9 + 5 + 7 = 31

FRAGMENTED DEATHDAY # '-NUMBER = 6 + 4 + 2 + 0 + 1 + 8 = 21

(31 + 21) = 52 = "SEE '-BELOW"!!!~'

(31 /|\ 21) = (3 + 1 + 2) (1) = 61 = AGE of DEATH for AMERICAN FOOTBALL PLAYER DWIGHT EDWARD CLARK!!!~'

WAS '-MARRIED to KELLY RADZIKOWSKI from 2011 TO 2018 = 7 YEARS = (6 + 1) = 61 = AGE of DEATH for AMERICAN FOOTBALL PLAYER DWIGHT EDWARD CLARK!!!~'

'-NUMBER 87 /|\ SAN FRANCISCO 49ERS / WIDE RECEIVER = "FLIP EVERY ('-8) OVER to a ('-3)"; "FLIP EVERY ('-7) OVER to a ('-2)" = ('-32) = -a PROPHETIC # '-NUMBER!!!~'

'-PLAYED ('-134) '-GAMES = (13 x 4) = 52 = "FLIP EVERY ('-2) OVER to a ('-7)" = 57 = BIRTH/YEAR!!!~'

FROM BIRTH-TO-DEATH there are 147 DAYS = (1 + 4) (7) = ('-57) = BIRTH/YEAR!!!~'

(365 (-) 147) = 218 = (2 – 8) (1) = 61 = AGE of DEATH for AMERICAN FOOTBALL PLAYER DWIGHT EDWARD CLARK!!!~'

BIRTH/MONTH = JANUARY = 31 DAYS!!!~'

(31 (-) 8) – (DAY of BIRTH) = 23 = -a PROPHETIC # `-NUMBER!!!~'

DEATH/DAY # `-NUMBER = 48 = (4 x 8) = 32 = -a PROPHETIC # `-NUMBER = "FLIP EVERY (`-3) OVER to an (`-8)"; "FLIP EVERY (`-2) OVER to a (`-7)" = 87 = `-NUMBER 87 /|\ SAN FRANCISCO 49ERS / WIDE RECEIVER!!!~'

BIRTH/DAY = 1/8 = DEATH/YEAR = 18!!!~'

AMERICAN STUNT PERFORMER ROBERT CRAIG "EVEL" KNIEVEL died at the AGE of 69!!!~'

BIRTHDAY # `-NUMBER = 10/17/19/38 = 10 + 17 + 19 + 38 = 84

DEATHDAY # `=NUMBER = 11/30/20/07 = 11 + 30 + 20 + 07 = 68

(84 + 68) = 152 = "FLIP EVERY (`-2) OVER to a (`-7)" = 157 = (57 x 1) = 57 = BIRTH/YEAR = (19 + 38) = 57!!!~'

DEATH/DAY # `-NUMBER = 68 = (6 x 8) = 48 = RECIPROCAL = 84 = BIRTH/DAY # `-NUMBER!!!~'

BIRTH/DAY = 10/17 (+) DEATH/DAY = 11/30 /|\ (10 + 17 + 11 + 30) = 68 = DEATH/DAY # `-NUMBER!!!~'

BIRTH/DAY = 10/17 = (10 – 17) = 7

DEATH/DAY = 11/30 = (11 – 30) = 19

(7/19) = (7 – 1) (9) = 69 = AGE of DEATH for AMERICAN STUNT PERFORMER ROBERT CRAIG "EVEL" KNIEVEL!!!~'

FRAGMENTED BIRTHDAY # '-NUMBER = 1 + 0 + 1 + 7 + 1 + 9 + 3 + 8 = 30

FRAGMENTED DEATHDAY # '-NUMBER = 1 + 1 + 3 + 0 + 2 + 0 + 0 + 7 = 14

(30 + 14) = 44 = DAYS from BIRTH-TO-DEATH!!!~'

WAS '-MARRIED to KRYSTAL KENNEDY from 1999 TO 2001 for 2 YEARS!!!~'

WAS '-MARRIED to LINDA KNIEVEL from 1959 TO 1997 for 38 YEARS = 38 = BIRTH/YEAR!!!~'

YEARS '-MARRIED = (2 x 38) = 76 = (7 x 6) = 42 (X TIMES) ('-2) = 84 = BIRTH/DAY # '-NUMBER!!!~'

('-38) = (3 x 8) = 24 = RECIPROCAL = 42 (X TIMES) ('-2) = 84 = BIRTH/DAY # '-NUMBER!!!~'

FIRST '-MARRIAGE '-STARTED in = (19/59) = (19 + 59) = 78

FIRST '-MARRIAGE '-ENDED in (19/97) = (97 (-) 19) = 78

BIRTH/DAY = 10/17 = HALF RECIPROCAL = 10/71 = (10 + 71) = 81

DEATH/DAY = 11/30 = (11 + 30) = 41

(81 + 41) = 122 = (1 + 22) = ('-23) = -a PROPHETIC # '-NUMBER!!!~'

FROM BIRTH-TO-DEATH there are 44 DAYS = FRAG BIRTH/ DEATH DAYS '-ADDED '-UP '-TOGETHER!!!~'

(365 (-) 44) = 321 = RECIPROCAL = 123 = Prophetic/Linear/ Progression-PLP!!!~'

(365 (-) 44) = 321 = "FLIP EVERY ('-3) OVER to an ('-8)" = 821 = (82 + 1) = 83 = RECIPROCAL = 38 = BIRTH/YEAR!!!~'

BIRTH/YEAR = 19/38 = (1 – 3 – 8) (9) = 69 = AGE of DEATH for AMERICAN STUNT PERFORMER ROBERT CRAIG "EVEL" KNIEVEL!!!~'

BIRTH/DAY = 10/17 = (10 + 17) = 27 = DEATH/YEAR = (20 + 07) = 27

(27 + 27) = 54 = (6 X 9) = AGE of DEATH for AMERICAN STUNT PERFORMER ROBERT CRAIG "EVEL" KNIEVEL!!!~'

HUNGARIAN-AMERICAN ESCAPE ARTIST HARRY HOUDINI died at the AGE of 52!!!~'

BIRTHDAY # '-NUMBER = 3/24/18/74 = 3 + 24 + 18 + 74 = 119

DEATHDAY # '-NUMBER = 10/31/19/26 = 10 + 31 + 19 + 26 = 86

(119 + 86) = 205 = (20 + 5) = 25 = RECIPROCAL = 52 = AGE of DEATH for HUNGARIAN-AMERICAN ESCAPE ARTIST HARRY HOUDINI!!!~'

BIRTH/DAY # '-NUMBER = 119 = RECIPROCAL = 911 = (91 x 1) = 91 = DEATH/DAY = 10/31 = "FLIP EVERY ('-3) OVER to an ('-8)" = 10/81 = (10 + 81) = 91!!!~'

BIRTH/DAY = 3/24 = HALF RECIPROCAL = 3/42 = (3 + 42) = 45 = DEATH/YEAR = (19 + 26) = 45!!!~'

BIRTH/DAY = 3/24 = (3 - 24) = 21

DEATH/DAY = 10/31 = (10 – 31) = 21

BIRTH/DAY = 3/24 = (3 + 24) = 27 = (9 X 3) = DEATH/YEAR = 19/26 = (9) (1 + 2 – 6) = 93

BIRTH/YEAR = 18/74 = (18 + 74) = 92 = RECIPROCAL = 29

BIRTH/DAY # `-NUMBER in REVERSE = (74 (-) 18 (-) 24 (-) 3) = 29

FRAGMENTED BIRTHDAY # `-NUMBER = 3 + 2 + 4 + 1 + 8 + 7 + 4 = 29

FRAGMENTED BIRTH/DAY # `-NUMBER = 29 = BIRTH/DAY # `-NUMBER = 119 = (1 + 1) (9) = 29 = "FLIP EVERY (`-9) OVER to a (`-6)" = 26 = DEATH/YEAR!!!~'

BIRTH/DAY # `-NUMBER = 119 = RECIPROCAL = 911 = (91 + 1) = 92 = RECIPROCAL = 29!!!~'

DEATH/DAY = 10/31 = HALF RECIPROCAL = 10/13 = (10 + 13) = 23 = -a PROPHETIC # `-NUMBER = RECIPROCAL = 32 = "SEE `-BELOW"!!!~'

FRAGMENTED DEATHDAY # `-NUMBER = 1 + 0 + 3 + 1 + 1 + 9 + 2 + 6 = 23

FRAGMENTED DEATH/DAY # `-NUMBER = 23 = RECIPROCAL = 32 = WAS `-MARRIED for (`-32) YEARS = "SEE `-ABOVE & `-BELOW"!!!~'

(29 + 23) = 52 = AGE of DEATH for HUNGARIAN-AMERICAN ESCAPE ARTIST HARRY HOUDINI!!!~'

WAS `-MARRIED to BESS HOUDINI from 1894 to 1926 = (`-32) = -a PROPHETIC # `-NUMBER = "SEE `-ABOVE & `-BELOW"!!!~'

FIRST `-MARRIED in 1894 = (18 + 94) = 112 / (DIVIDED by) (`-2) = 56

(18 – 94) = 76 = (7 + 6) = 13 = RECIPROCAL = 31 = DAY of `-DEATH!!!~'

FROM BIRTH-TO-DEATH there are 144 DAYS = (14 x 4) = 56 = BIRTH/YEAR = (18 – 74) = 56!!!~'

(365 (-) 144) = 221 = (22 + 1) = 23 = -a PROPHETIC # `-NUMBER = RECIPROCAL = 32 = MARRIED for (`-32) YEARS!!!~'

(365 (-) 144) = 221 = (2 + 2) (1) = 41 = DEATH/DAY = 10/31 = (10 + 31) = 41

BIRTH/DAY = 3/24 (+) DEATH/DAY = 10/31 /|\ (3 + 24 + 10 + 31) = 68 = RECIPROCAL = 86 = DEATH/DAY # `-NUMBER!!!~'

DEATH/YEAR = 19/26 = (1 – 6) (9 – 2) = 57 = "FLIP EVERY (`-7) OVER to a (`-2)" = 52 = AGE of DEATH for HUNGARIAN-AMERICAN ESCAPE ARTIST HARRY HOUDINI!!!~'

DEATH/YEAR = 19/26 = (1 – 6) (9 + 2) = (5) (11) = (5) (1 + 1) = 52 = AGE of DEATH for HUNGARIAN-AMERICAN ESCAPE ARTIST HARRY HOUDINI!!!~'

BIRTH/MONTH = MARCH = 31 DAYS!!!~'

(31 (-) 24) – (DAY of BIRTH) = 7 = (5 + 2) = 52 = AGE of DEATH for HUNGARIAN-AMERICAN ESCAPE ARTIST HARRY HOUDINI!!!~'

AMERICAN BLUES SINGER/SONGWRITER (B.B. KING) RILEY B. KING died at the AGE of 89!!!~

BIRTH/DAY = 9/16 = (9 – 1) (6) = 86 = "FLIP EVERY (`-6) OVER to a (`-9)" = 89 = AGE of DEATH for AMERICAN BLUES SINGER/ SONGWRITER (B.B. KING) RILEY B. KING!!!~'

BIRTHDAY # `-NUMBER = 9/16/19/25 = 9 + 16 + 19 + 25 = 69

BIRTH/DAY # `-NUMBER = 69 = BIRTH/DAY = 9/16 = (96 x 1) = 96 = RECIPROCAL = 69

DEATHDAY # `-NUMBER = 5/14/20/15 = 5 + 14 + 20 + 15 = 54

DEATH/DAY # `-NUMBER = 54 = (6 X 9) = BIRTH/DAY # `-NUMBER!!!~'

(69 + 54) = 123 = Prophetic/Linear/Progression-PLP!!!~'

(69 (-) 54) = 15 = DEATH/YEAR!!!~'

DEATH/DAY # `-NUMBER = 54 = DEATH/DAY = 5/14 = (54 x 1) = 54

BIRTH/DAY = 9/16 = (9 + 16) = 25 = BIRTH/YEAR!!!~'

BIRTH/DAY = 9/16 = (9 – 16) = 7

DEATH/DAY = 5/14 = (5 – 14) = 9

(7/9) = (7 x 9) = 63 = "FLIP EVERY (`-3) OVER to an (`-8)" = 68 = RECIPROCAL = 86 = "FLIP EVERY (`-6) OVER to a (`-9)" = 89 =

AGE of DEATH for AMERICAN BLUES SINGER/SONGWRITER (B.B. KING) RILEY B. KING!!!~'

FRAGMENTED BIRTHDAY # `-NUMBER = 9 + 1 + 6 + 1 + 9 + 2 + 5 = 33

FRAGMENTED DEATHDAY # `-NUMBER = 5 + 1 + 4 + 2 + 0 + 1 + 5 = 18

(33/18) = (3 + 3) (1 x 8) = 68 = RECIPROCAL = 86 = "FLIP EVERY (`-6) OVER to a (`-9)" = 89 = AGE of DEATH for AMERICAN BLUES SINGER/SONGWRITER (B.B. KING) RILEY B. KING!!!~'

(33 (-) 18) = 15 = DEATH/YEAR!!!~'

WAS `-MARRIED to SUE CAROL HALL from 19(58) TO 19(66) = 8 YEARS!!!~'

START of 2ND MARRIAGE = 19(58) = (58 (-) 19) = 39 = "FLIP EVERY (`-3) OVER to an (`-8)" = 89 = AGE of DEATH for AMERICAN BLUES SINGER/SONGWRITER (B.B. KING) RILEY B. KING!!!~'

END of 2ND `-MARRIAGE = (1966) = (19 + 66) = 85 = RECIPROCAL = 58 = WAS THE `-START of 2ND `-MARRIAGE!!!~'

DEATH/YEAR = (20 + 15) = 35 = "FLIP EVERY (`-3) OVER to an (`-8)" = 85

WAS `-MARRIED to MARTHA LEE DENTON from 19(46) TO 19(52) = 6 YEARS!!!~'

FIRST `-MARRIAGE STARTED in (`-46) = DEATH/DAY = 5/14 = (5 + 1) (4) = 64 = RECIPROCAL = (`-46)!!!~'

FIRST `-MARRIAGE ENDED in (`-52) = RECIPROCAL = (`-25) = BIRTH/YEAR!!!~'

YEARS `-MARRIED (8/6) = "FLIP EVERY (`-6) OVER to a (`-9)" = 89 = AGE of DEATH for AMERICAN BLUES SINGER/SONGWRITER (B.B. KING) RILEY B. KING!!!~'

FROM BIRTH-TO-DEATH there are 125 DAYS = (1 x 25) = 25 = BIRTH/YEAR!!!~'

(365 (-) 125) = 240 = (24 + 0) = 24 = (6 X 4) = RECIPROCAL = (`-46) = WAS `-FIRST `-MARRIED in (`-46)!!!~'

(365 (-) 125) = 240 = (24 + 0) = 24 = (6 X 4) = DEATH/DAY = 5/14 = (5 + 1) (4) = (`-64)!!!~'

DEATH/MONTH = MAY = 31 DAYS!!!~'

(31 (-) 14) – (DAY of DEATH) = 17 = (8 + 9) = AGE of DEATH for AMERICAN BLUES SINGER/SONGWRITER (B.B. KING) RILEY B. KING!!!~'

BIRTH/DAY = 9/16 (+) DEATH/DAY = 5/14 /|\ (9 + 16 + 5 + 14) = 44 = BIRTH/YEAR = (19 + 25) = (`-44)!!!

(44 + 44) = 88 = (8 x 8) = (`-64) = DEATH/DAY = 5/14 = (5 + 1) (4) = (`-64)!!!~'

BIRTH/YEAR = 19/25 = (9) (1 + 2 + 5) = 98 = RECIPROCAL = 89 = AGE of DEATH for AMERICAN BLUES SINGER/SONGWRITER (B.B. KING) RILEY B. KING!!!~'

AMERICAN SOUL AND R&B SINGER/RECORD PRODUCER BENJAMIN EARL KING died at the AGE of 76!!!~'

BIRTH/YEAR = 38 = (3 x 8) = 24 = RECIPROCAL = 42 = (7 X 6) = AGE of DEATH for AMERICAN SOUL AND R&B SINGER/ RECORD PRODUCER BENJAMIN EARL KING!!!~'

BIRTH/YEAR = **1**9/3**8** = (1 – 8) (9 – 3) = 76 = AGE of DEATH for AMERICAN SOUL AND R&B SINGER/RECORD PRODUCER BENJAMIN EARL KING!!!~'

BIRTHDAY # `-NUMBER = 9/28/19/38 = 9 + 28 + 19 + 38 = 94

BIRTH/DAY # `-NUMBER = 94 = (9 x 4) = 36 = RECIPROCAL = 63 = (7 X 9) = "FLIP EVERY (`-9) OVER to a (`-6)" = 76 = AGE of DEATH for AMERICAN SOUL AND R&B SINGER/RECORD PRODUCER BENJAMIN EARL KING!!!~'

DEATHDAY # `-NUMBER = 4/30/20/15 = 4 + 30 + 20 + 15 = 69

(94 + 69) = 163 = (1 x 63) = 63 = (7 X 9) = "FLIP EVERY (`-9) OVER to a (`-6)" = 76 = AGE of DEATH for AMERICAN SOUL AND R&B SINGER/RECORD PRODUCER BENJAMIN EARL KING!!!~'

(94 (-) 69) = 25 = DEATH/YEAR = **2**0/1**5** = (25 x 1 + 0) = (`-25)!!!~'

WAS `-BORN in the `-MONTH (`-9); AND, `-DIED in the `-MONTH of (`-4) = 9/4 = BIRTH/DAY # `-NUMBER = (`-94)!!!~'

(9 + 4) = 13 = (7 + 6) = 76 = AGE of DEATH for AMERICAN SOUL AND R&B SINGER/RECORD PRODUCER BENJAMIN EARL KING!!!~'

(`-94) = (9 x 4) = 36 = RECIPROCAL = 63 = (7 X 9) = "FLIP EVERY (`-9) OVER to a (`-6)" = 76 = AGE of DEATH for AMERICAN

SOUL AND R&B SINGER/RECORD PRODUCER BENJAMIN EARL KING!!!~'

BIRTH/DAY = 9/28 = (9 x 28) = 252 = (2 + 52) = 54 = (6 X 9) = DEATH/DAY # `-NUMBER!!!~'

DEATH/DAY = 4/30 = (4 – 30) = 26 = "FLIP EVERY (`-2) OVER to a (`-7)" = 76 = AGE of DEATH for AMERICAN SOUL AND R&B SINGER/RECORD PRODUCER BENJAMIN EARL KING!!!~'

DAY of `-BIRTH = 28th = 2(8's) = 88 = DEATH/YEAR = (20 + 15) = 35 = RECIPROCAL = 53!!!~'

(35 + 53) = (`-88)!!!~'

FRAGMENTED BIRTHDAY # `-NUMBER = 9 + 2 + 8 + 1 + 9 + 3 + 8 = 40

FRAGMENTED DEATHDAY # `-NUMBER = 4 + 3 + 0 + 2 + 0 + 1 + 5 = 15

(40/15) = (4 + 0) (1 x 5) = 45 = RECIPROCAL = 54 = (6 X 9) = DEATH/DAY # `-NUMBER!!!~'

(40 + 15) = 55 = (5 x 5) = 25 = DEATH/YEAR = 2̲0/1̲5̲ = (25 x 1 + 0) = (`-25)!!!~'

FRAGMENTED DEATH/DAY # `-NUMBER = 15 = DEATH/YEAR = 15 = RECIPROCAL = 51 = WAS `-MARRIED for (`-51) YEARS!!!~'

WAS `-MARRIED to BETTY KING from 1964 to 2015 = 51 YEARS = RECIPROCAL = 15 = DEATH/YEAR = (`-15)!!!~'

FIRST `-MARRIED in (19/64) = (19 + 64) = 83 = (8 x 3) = 24 = RECIPROCAL = 42 = (7 X 6) = AGE of DEATH for AMERICAN

SOUL AND R&B SINGER/RECORD PRODUCER BENJAMIN EARL KING!!!~'

('-15) = RECIPROCAL = ('-51)

FROM BIRTH-TO-DEATH there are 151 DAYS = (1 x 51) = 51 = MARRIED for ('-51) YEARS = RECIPROCAL = ('-15) = DEATH/ YEAR!!!~'

(365 (-) 151) = 214 = (24 x 1) = 24 = RECIPROCAL = 42 = (7 X 6) = AGE of DEATH for AMERICAN SOUL AND R&B SINGER/ RECORD PRODUCER BENJAMIN EARL KING!!!~'

AMERICAN LAWYER AND POLITICIAN EDWARD MOORE KENNEDY died at the AGE of 77!!!~'

BIRTH/DAY = 2/22 (+) DEATH/DAY = 8/25 /|\ (2 + 22 + 8 + 25) = 57 = RECIPROCAL = 75 = BIRTH/DAY # '-NUMBER!!!~'

BIRTHDAY # '-NUMBER = 2/22/19/32 = 2 + 22 + 19 + 32 = 75

BIRTH/DAY # '-NUMBER = 75 = "FLIP EVERY ('-7) OVER to a ('-2)" = 25 = DAY of '-DEATH!!!~'

DEATHDAY # '-NUMBER = 8/25/20/09 = 8 + 25 + 20 + 09 = 62

(75 + 62) = 137 = RECIPROCAL = 731 = (7) (3 + 1) = ('-74)!!!~'

(75 + 62) = 137 = (1 x 37) = 37 = RECIPROCAL = 73 = ONE '-MARRIAGE '-STARTED in (1992) = (19 – 92) = ('-73)!!!~'

BIRTH/YEAR = ('-**32**) = -a PROPHETIC # '-NUMBER!!!~'

BIRTH/MONTH = FEBRUARY = 28 DAYS!!!~'

(28 (-) 22) – (DAY of BIRTH) = ('-**6**)!!!~'

DEATH/MONTH = AUGUST = 31 DAYS!!!~'

(31 (-) 25) – (DAY of DEATH) = ('-**6**)!!!~'

DEATH/DAY = 8/25 = (8 + 25) = 33 (X TIMES) ('-2) = ('-**66**)!!!~'

FRAGMENTED BIRTHDAY # '-NUMBER = 2 + 2 + 2 + 1 + 9 + 3 + 2 = 21

FRAGMENTED DEATHDAY # '-NUMBER = 8 + 2 + 5 + 2 + 0 + 0 + 9 = 26

FRAGMENTED DEATH/DAY # '-NUMBER = 26 = RECIPROCAL = 62 = DEATH/DAY # '-NUMBER!!!~'

(21 + 26) = ('-47) = BIRTH/YEAR = 19/32 = (1 + 3) (9 – 2) = ('-47)!!!~'

WAS '-MARRIED to VICTORIA REGGIE KENNEDY from (1992) TO (2009) = 17 YEARS = DEATH/DAY = 8/25 = (8 – 25) = ('-17)!!!~'

WAS '-MARRIED to VICTORIA REGGIE KENNEDY from (1992) TO (2009) = 17 YEARS = RECIPROCAL = 71 = FLIP EVERY ('-7) OVER to a ('-2)" = 21 = FRAGMENTED BIRTH/DAY # '-NUMBER!!!~'

'-MARRIED in ('-92); AND, MARRIAGE '-ENDED in = RECIPROCAL = (2)00(9) =

'-MARRIAGE '-ENDED in (2009) = (20 + 09) = ('-29)!!!~'

$(29 + 29) = (`-58) = $ YEAR `-FIRST `-MARRIED!!!~'

WAS `-MARRIED to JOAN BENNETT KENNEDY from (1958) TO (1982) = 24 YEARS = BIRTH/DAY = 2/22 = (2 + 22) = 24

FROM BIRTH-TO-DEATH there are 184 DAYS = RECIPROCAL = 481 = (48 + 1) = 49 = (7 X 7) = AGE of DEATH for AMERICAN LAWYER AND POLITICIAN EDWARD MOORE KENNEDY!!!~'

$(365 (-) 184) = 181 = (18 - 1) = 17 = $ LENGTH in YEARS Of `-ONE `-MARRIAGE!!!~'

$(365 (-) 184) = 181 = (1 + 81) = 82 = $ FIRST `-MARRIAGE `-ENDED!!!~'

WAS `-FIRST `-MARRIED in $(19/58) = (19 + 58) = 77 = $ AGE of DEATH for AMERICAN LAWYER AND POLITICIAN EDWARD MOORE KENNEDY!!!~'

AMERICAN LAWYER AND POLITICIAN ROBERT FRANCIS KENNEDY died at the AGE of 42!!!~'

BIRTH/DAY = 11/20 (+) DEATH/DAY = 6/6 /|\ $(11 + 20 + 6 + 6)$ = 43 = DIED within HIS (`-43$^{rd}$) YEAR of `-EXISTENCE!!!~'

BIRTHDAY # `-NUMBER = 11/20/19/25 = 11 + 20 + 19 + 25 = 75

DEATHDAY # `-NUMBER = 6/6/19/68 = 6 + 6 + 19 + 68 = 99

$(99 (-) 75) = 24 = $ RECIPROCAL = 42 = AGE of DEATH for AMERICAN LAWYER AND POLITICIAN ROBERT FRANCIS KENNEDY!!!~'

$(99 + 75) = 174 = (1 + 74) = 75 = $ BIRTH/DAY # `-NUMBER!!!~'

DEATH/DAY = 6/6 = "FLIP EVERY (`-6) OVER to a (`-9)" = 99 = DEATH/DAY # `-NUMBER!!!~'

DEATH/DAY # `-NUMBER in `-REVERSE = (68 (-) 19 (-) 6 (-) 6) = 37 = (3 x 7) = 21 (X TIMES) (`-2) = 42 = AGE of DEATH for AMERICAN LAWYER AND POLITICIAN ROBERT FRANCIS KENNEDY!!!~'

BIRTH/DAY = 11/20 = (11 + 20) = 31 = RECIPROCAL = 13 = (6 + 7) = (6 x 7) = 42 = AGE of DEATH for AMERICAN LAWYER AND POLITICIAN ROBERT FRANCIS KENNEDY!!!~'

DEATH/DAY = 6/6 = (6 x 6) = 36 = (7 x 9) = "FLIP EVERY (`-9) OVER to a (`-6)" = (7 x 6) = 42 = AGE of DEATH for AMERICAN LAWYER AND POLITICIAN ROBERT FRANCIS KENNEDY!!!~'

DEATH/MONTH = JUNE = 30 DAYS!!!~'

(30 (-) 6) – (DAY of DEATH) = 24 = RECIPROCAL = 42 = AGE of DEATH for AMERICAN LAWYER AND POLITICIAN ROBERT FRANCIS KENNEDY!!!~'

FRAGMENTED BIRTHDAY # `-NUMBER = 1 + 1 + 2 + 0 + 1 + 9 + 2 + 5 = 21

FRAGMENTED BIRTH/DAY # `-NUMBER = 21 (X TIMES) (`-2) = 42 = AGE of DEATH for AMERICAN LAWYER AND POLITICIAN ROBERT FRANCIS KENNEDY!!!~'

FRAGMENTED DEATHDAY # `-NUMBER = 6 + 6 + 1 + 9 + 6 + 8 = 36

FRAGMENTED DEATH/DAY # `-NUMBER = 36 = (7 x 9) = "FLIP EVERY (`-9) OVER to a (`-6)" = (7 x 6) = 42 = AGE of DEATH for

AMERICAN LAWYER AND POLITICIAN ROBERT FRANCIS
KENNEDY!!!~'

(21/36) = (2) (1 – 3 – 6) = 24 = RECIPROCAL = 42 = AGE of
DEATH for AMERICAN LAWYER AND POLITICIAN ROBERT
FRANCIS KENNEDY!!!~'

MARRIED (19/50) = (19 + 50) = 69 = "FLIP EVERY (`-6) OVER to
a (`-9)" = 99 = DEATH/DAY # `-NUMBER!!!~'

WAS `-MARRIED to ETHEL KENNEDY from (1950) TO (1968)
= 18 YEARS = (6 X 3) = "FLIP EVERY (`-3) OVER to an (`-8)" = 68
= DEATH/YEAR!!!~'

`-MARRIED in 1950 = (19 – 50) = 31 = BIRTH/DAY = 11/20 = (11
+ 20) = 31

FROM BIRTH-TO-DEATH there are 167 DAYS = (1 x 67) = 67 =
(6 x 7) = 42 = AGE of DEATH for AMERICAN LAWYER AND
POLITICIAN ROBERT FRANCIS KENNEDY!!!~'

(365 (-) 167) = 198 = (1 x 98) = 98 = "FLIP EVERY (`-9) OVER to a
(`-6)" = 68 = DEATH/DAY # `-NUMBER!!!~'

BIRTH/YEAR = 19/25 = (1 x 2) (9 – 5) = 24 = RECIPROCAL = 42
= AGE of DEATH for AMERICAN LAWYER AND POLITICIAN
ROBERT FRANCIS KENNEDY!!!~'

DEATH/YEAR = 19/68 = (1 – 9) (6 + 8) = (8) (14) = (84 x 1) = 84
/ (DIVIDED by) (`-2) = 42 = AGE of DEATH for AMERICAN
LAWYER AND POLITICIAN ROBERT FRANCIS KENNEDY!!!~'

FORMER FIRST LADY JACQUELINE LEE "JACKIE" KENNEDY ONASSIS died at the AGE of 64!!!~'

BIRTH/DAY = 7/28 = HALF RECIPROCAL = 7/82 = (7 – 82) = 75 = DEATH/YEAR = (19 – 94) = 75!!!~'

WAS '-BORN in the '-MONTH of ('-7); AND, '-DIED in the '-MONTH of ('-5) = ('-7/5)!!!~'

BIRTHDAY # '-NUMBER = 7/28/19/29 = 7 + 28 + 19 + 29 = 83

DEATHDAY # '-NUMBER = 5/19/19/94 = 5 + 19 + 19 + 94 = 137

DEATH/DAY # '-NUMBER = 137 = (1 + 37) = 38 = SON'S '-AGE of '-DEATH JOHN F. KENNEDY JR. = ('-38) = RECIPROCAL = ('-83) = BIRTH/DAY # '-NUMBER!!!~'

BIRTH/DAY = 7/28 = (7 + 28) = 35 = RECIPROCAL = 53 = WAS '-FIRST '-MARRIED to #35/PRESIDENT JOHN F. KENNEDY!!!~'

DEATH/DAY = 5/19 = "FLIP EVERY ('-9) OVER to a ('-6)" = 5/16 = (5 – 1) (6) = 46 = HUSBAND JOHN F. KENNEDY'S '-AGE of '-DEATH = RECIPROCAL = 64 = AGE of DEATH for FORMER FIRST LADY JACQUELINE LEE "JACKIE" KENNEDY ONASSIS!!!~'

DEATH/DAY = 5/19 = (5 – 1) (9) = 49 = RECIPROCAL = 94 = DEATH/YEAR!!!~'

DEATH/DAY = 5/19 = (5 – 1) (9) = 49 = RECIPROCAL = 94 = "FLIP EVERY ('-9) OVER to a ('-6) = 64 = AGE of DEATH for FORMER FIRST LADY JACQUELINE LEE "JACKIE" KENNEDY ONASSIS!!!~'

BIRTH/MONTH = JULY = 31 DAYS!!!~'

(31 (-) 28) – (DAY of BIRTH) = ('-**3**)!!!~'

DEATH/MONTH = MAY = 31 DAYS!!!~'

(31 (-) 19) – (DAY of DEATH) = (12) = (1 + 2) = ('-**3**)!!!~'

FRAGMENTED BIRTHDAY # '-NUMBER = 7 + 2 + 8 + 1 + 9 + 2 + 9 = 38

FRAGMENTED BIRTH/DAY # '-NUMBER = 38 = "SEE '-ABOVE for '-SON" = DEATH/DAY # '-NUMBER = 137 = (1 + 37) = 38 = RECIPROCAL = 83 = BIRTH/DAY # '-NUMBER!!!~'

FRAGMENTED DEATHDAY # '-NUMBER = 5 + 1 + 9 + 1 + 9 + 9 + 4 = 38

FRAGMENTED DEATH/DAY # '-NUMBER = 38 = FRAGMENTED BIRTH/DAY # '-NUMBER = 38 = "SEE '-ABOVE for '-SON" = DEATH/DAY # '-NUMBER = 137 = (1 + 37) = 38 = RECIPROCAL = 83 = BIRTH/DAY # '-NUMBER!!!~'

(38 + 38) = 76 = (7 x 6) = 42 = AGE of DEATH for AMERICAN LAWYER AND POLITICIAN ROBERT FRANCIS KENNEDY!!!~'

WAS '-MARRIED to ARISTOTLE ONASSIS from 1968 to 1975 = 7 YEARS!!!~'

WAS '-MARRIED in (19/68) = (19 – 68) = 49 = RECIPROCAL = 94 = DEATH/YEAR = "SEE '-BELOW & ABOVE"!!!~'

MARRIAGE '-ENDED in (19/75) = (19 + 75) = 94 = DEATH/ YEAR!!!~'

MARRIAGE `-ENDED in (19/75) = (19 + 75) = 94 = "FLIP EVERY (`-9) OVER to a (`-6)" = 64 = AGE of DEATH for FORMER FIRST LADY JACQUELINE LEE "JACKIE" KENNEDY ONASSIS!!!~'

WAS `-MARRIED to #35/PRESIDENT JOHN F. KENNEDY from 1953 to 1963 = 10 YEARS = (6 + 4) = 64 = AGE of DEATH for FORMER FIRST LADY JACQUELINE LEE "JACKIE" KENNEDY ONASSIS!!!~'

FIRST `-MARRIED in (19/53) = (19 – 53) = 34 = AGE at TIME WHEN `-MARRIAGE `-ENDED by HUSBAND'S ASSASSINATION!!!~'

(19/63) = (19 + 63) = 82 = RECIPROCAL = 28 = DAY of `-BIRTH!!!~'

FROM BIRTH-TO-DEATH there are 70 DAYS = / (DIVIDED by) (`-2) = 35 = RECIPROCAL = 53 = WAS FIRST `-MARRIED in (`-53)!!!~'

(365 (-) 70) = 295 = (29 + 5) = 34 = AGE at WHAT TIME `-FIRST `-MARRIAGE `-ENDED by HUSBAND'S ASSASSINATION!!!~'

DEATH/DAY = 5/19 = (5 + 19) = 24 = RECIPROCAL = 42 = AGE of DEATH for AMERICAN LAWYER AND POLITICIAN ROBERT FRANCIS KENNEDY!!!~'

AGE of DEATH = 64 = (6 x 4) = 24 = RECIPROCAL = 42 = AGE of DEATH for AMERICAN LAWYER AND POLITICIAN ROBERT FRANCIS KENNEDY!!!~'

DEATH/YEAR = 19/94 = (9) (1 + 9 + 4) = (9) (14) = (94 x 1) = 94 = "FLIP EVERY (`-9) OVER to a (`-6)" = 64 = AGE of DEATH for FORMER FIRST LADY JACQUELINE LEE "JACKIE" KENNEDY ONASSIS!!!~'

35th PRESIDENT OF THE UNITED STATES of AMERICA JOHN FITZGERALD KENNEDY died at the AGE of 46!!!~'

BIRTH/YEAR = 19/17 = (19 + 17) = 36 = RECIPROCAL = 63 = DEATH/YEAR!!!~'

BIRTHDAY # `-NUMBER = 5/29/19/17 = 5 + 29 + 19 + 17 = 70

BIRTH/DAY # `-NUMBER = 70 / (DIVIDED by) (`-2) = 35 = HIS PRESIDENTIAL # `-NUMBER = RECIPROCAL = 53 = YEAR HE was `-MARRIED!!!~'

PART of BIRTH = (5 + 29 + 19) = 53 = YEAR of `-MARRIAGE = RECIPROCAL = 35 = HIS PRESIDENTIAL # `-NUMBER!!!~'

DEATHDAY # `-NUMBER = 11/22/19/63 = 11 + 22 + 19 + 63 = 115

WAS `-BORN in the `-MONTH of (`-5); AND, `-DIED in the `-MONTH of (`-11) = 5/11 = RECIPROCAL = 11/5 = DEATH/DAY # `-NUMBER!!!~'

DEATHDAY # `-NUMBER = 115 = (1 + 1) (5) = 25 = FRAGMENTED DEATH/DAY # `-NUMBER!!!~'

(70 + 115) = 185 = (1 x 85) = 85 = RECIPROCAL = 58 = "FLIP EVERY (`-8) OVER to a (`-3)" = 53 = WAS `-MARRIED in (`-53) = RECIPROCAL = 35 = HIS PRESIDENTIAL # `-NUMBER!!!~'

(115 (-) 70) = (`-45) = RECIPROCAL = (`-54)!!!~'

(45 + 54) = 99 / (DIVIDED by) (`-3) = 33 = DEATH/DAY = 11/22 = (11 + 22) = 33

BIRTH/DAY = 5/29 = (5 + 29) = 34 = AGE of WIFE JACQUELINE KENNEDY ONASSIS at TIME of HIS OWN `-ASSASSINATION!!!~'

DEATH/DAY = 11/22 = (11 x 22) = 242 = `-ASSASSINATION of `-HIS `-BROTHER ROBERT FRANCIS KENNEDY with HIS AGE of DEATH & the AGE of the ASSASSINATOR at TIME of ASSASSINATION which was 24 YEARS of AGE for SIRHAN BISHARA SIRHAN!!!~'

FRAGMENTED BIRTHDAY # `-NUMBER = 5 + 2 + 9 + 1 + 9 + 1 + 7 = 34 = AGE of WIFE JACQUELINE KENNEDY ONASSIS at TIME of HER HUSBAND JOHN F. KENNEDY'S ASSASSINATION!!!~'

FRAGMENTED DEATHDAY # `-NUMBER = 1 + 1 + 2 + 2 + 1 + 9 + 6 + 3 = 25

(34/25) = (ENCAPSULATED `-WITHIN) = `-AGE of `-DEATH of BROTHER= 42 = /|\ 35 = HIS PRESIDENTIAL # `-NUMBER = RECIPROCAL = 53 = YEAR of MARRIAGE!!!~'

WAS `-MARRIED to JACQUELINE KENNEDY ONASSIS from 1953 to 1963 = 10 YEARS = (4 + 6) = AGE of DEATH for 35th PRESIDENT OF THE UNITED STATES of AMERICA JOHN FITZGERALD KENNEDY!!!~'

YEAR of `-MARRIAGE = (19 – 53) = 34 = AGE of HIS WIFE JACQUELINE KENNEDY ONASSIS at the TIME of HIS JOHN F. KENNEDY'S `-ASSASSINATION!!!~'

FROM BIRTH-TO-DEATH there are 177 DAYS = (17 + 7) = 24 = RECIPROCAL = 42 = AGE of DEATH for AMERICAN LAWYER AND POLITICIAN ROBERT FRANCIS KENNEDY!!!~'

$(365 \, (\text{-}) \, 177) = 188 = (18 \, (\text{-}) \, 8) = 10 = (4 + 6) = $ AGE of DEATH for 35ᵗʰ PRESIDENT OF THE UNITED STATES of AMERICA JOHN FITZGERALD KENNEDY!!!~'

AGE of DEATH (HUSBAND) JFK = 46 = RECIPROCAL = 64 = AGE of DEATH (WIFE)!!!~'

AMERICAN BAPTIST MINISTER AND ACTIVIST MARTIN LUTHER KING JR. died at the AGE of 39!!!~'

DEATH/YEAR = 19/68 = (19 + 68) = 87 = RECIPROCAL = 78 = AGE of DEATH for WIFE AMERICAN AUTHOR, ACTIVIST, CIVIL RIGHTS LEADER CORETTA SCOTT KING!!!~'

BIRTH/YEAR = 19/29 = (19 + 29) = 48 = (4 x 8) = 32 = FRAGMENTED DEATH/DAY # `-NUMBER!!!~'

BIRTHDAY # `-NUMBER = 1/15/19/29 = 1 + 15 + 19 + 29 = 64

DEATHDAY # `-NUMBER = 4/4/19/68 = 4 + 4 + 19 + 68 = 95

$(64/95) = (6 - 9) (4 + 5) = 39 = $ AGE of DEATH for AMERICAN BAPTIST MINISTER AND ACTIVIST MARTIN LUTHER KING JR.!!!~'

$(64 + 95) = 159 = (1 \times 59) = 59 = $ RECIPROCAL = 95 = DEATH/DAY # `-NUMBER!!!~'

$(95 \, (\text{-}) \, 64) = 31 = $ RECIPROCAL = 13 = "A VERY PIVOTAL # `-NUMBER" = RECIPROCAL = 31 = WIFE'S DEATH/DAY = 1/30 = (1 + 30) = (`-31)!!!~'

BIRTH/DAY = 1/15 = (1 + 15) = 16 = (4 X 4) = DEATH/DAY!!!~'

FRAGMENTED BIRTHDAY # `-NUMBER = 1 + 1 + 5 + 1 + 9 + 2 + 9 = 28

FRAGMENTED BIRTH/DAY # `-NUMBER = 28 = RECIPROCAL = 82 = "FLIP EVERY (`-2) OVER to a (`-7)" = 87 = (19 + 68) = DEATH/YEAR!!!~'

FRAGMENTED BIRTH/DAY # `-NUMBER = 28 = RECIPROCAL = 82 = "FLIP EVERY (`-8) OVER to a (`-3)" = 32 = FRAGMENTED DEATH/DAY # `-NUMBER!!!~'

FRAGMENTED DEATHDAY # `-NUMBER = 4 + 4 + 1 + 9 + 6 + 8 = 32

FRAGMENTED DEATH/DAY # `-NUMBER = 32 = -a PROPHETIC # `-NUMBER!!!~'

(28/32) = (2 + 8) (3 + 2) = (10) (5) = (10 + 5) = 15 = WAS `-MARRIED for (`-15) YEARS!!!~'

BIRTH/MONTH = JANUARY = 31 DAYS!!!~'

(31 (-) 15) – (DAY of BIRTH) = 16 = (4 X 4) = DEATH/DAY!!!~'

DEATH/MONTH = APRIL = 30 DAYS!!!~'

(30 (-) 4) – (DAY of DEATH) = 26 = BIRTH/DAY = 1/15 = RECIPROCAL = 51/1 = (51 + 1) = 52 / (DIVIDED by) (`-2) = (`-26)!!!~'

DEATH/MONTH = APRIL = 30 DAYS!!!~'

(30 (-) 4) – (DAY of DEATH) = 26 = "FLIP EVERY (`-6) OVER to a (`-9)" = 29 = BIRTH/YEAR!!!~'

WAS `-MARRIED to CORETTA SCOTT KING from 1953 to 1968
= 15 YEARS = BIRTH/DAY = 1/15 = (1 x 15) = 15!!!~'

`-MARRIED in (19/53) = (19 + 53) = 72 = RECIPROCAL = 27 =
(3 X 9) = AGE of DEATH for AMERICAN BAPTIST MINISTER
AND ACTIVIST MARTIN LUTHER KING JR.!!!~'

FROM BIRTH-TO-DEATH there are 79 DAYS = (7 x 9) = 63 =
RECIPROCAL = 36 = (19 – 55) = WHEN `-HE WAS `-UNDERWAY
in the CIVIL RIGHTS MOVEMENT!!!~'

FROM BIRTH-TO-DEATH there are 79 DAYS = 79 / (DIVIDED
by) (`-2) = 39.5 = AGE of DEATH for AMERICAN BAPTIST
MINISTER AND ACTIVIST MARTIN LUTHER KING JR.!!!~'

FROM BIRTH-TO-DEATH there are 79 DAYS = WIFE
CORETTA SCOTT KING `-DIED within `-HER (79th) YEAR of
EXISTENCE!!!~'

(365 (-) 79) = 286 = (2 x 86) = 172 = (1 x 72) = 72 = RECIPROCAL
= 27 = (3 X 9) = AGE of DEATH for AMERICAN BAPTIST
MINISTER AND ACTIVIST MARTIN LUTHER KING JR.!!!~'

BIRTH/YEAR = 19/29 = (1 + 2) (99) = (3) (99) = AGE of DEATH for
AMERICAN BAPTIST MINISTER AND ACTIVIST MARTIN
LUTHER KING JR.!!!~'

BIRTH/YEAR = 19/29 = (9) (1 + 2 + 9) = (9) (12) = (9) (1 + 2) = (`-
93) = RECIPROCAL = (`-39) = AGE of DEATH for AMERICAN
BAPTIST MINISTER AND ACTIVIST MARTIN LUTHER
KING JR.!!!~'

DEATH/YEAR = 19/68 = (19 – 68) = 49 = (4 x 9) = 36 = "FLIP EVERY
(`-6) OVER to a (`-9)" = 39 = AGE of DEATH for AMERICAN

BAPTIST MINISTER AND ACTIVIST MARTIN LUTHER KING JR.!!!~'

WAS `-BORN in the `-MONTH of (`-1); AND, `-DIED in the `-MONTH of (`-4) = 1/4 = RECIPROCAL = 4/1 = DEATH/DAY # `-NUMBER in `-REVERSE = (68 (-) 19 (-) 4 (-) 4) = (`-41)!!!~'

WIFE CORETTA SCOTT KING was `-BORN in the `-MONTH of (`-4); AND, `-DIED in the `-MONTH of (`-1) = 4/1 = DEATH/ DAY # `-NUMBER in `-REVERSE = (68 (-) 19 (-) 4 (-) 4) = (`-41) for MARTIN LUTHER KING JR.!!!~'

AMERICAN AUTHOR, ACTIVIST, CIVIL RIGHTS LEADER; AND, WIFE of MARTIN LUTHER KING JR. CORETTA SCOTT KING died at the AGE of 78!!!~'

`-DAY of `-BIRTH (`-27th) = YEAR of `-BIRTH = (`-27)!!!~'

BIRTH/DAY = 4/27 (+) DEATH/DAY = 1/30 /|\ (4 + 27 + 1 + 30) = 62 = RECIPROCAL = 26 = DEATH/YEAR = (20 + 06) = 26!!!~'

BIRTHDAY # `-NUMBER = 4/27/19/27 = 4 + 27 + 19 + 27 = 77

BIRTHDAY # `-NUMBER = 77 = (7 x 7) = 49 = (19 – 68) = DEATH/ YEAR of `-HUSBAND AMERICAN BAPTIST MINISTER AND ACTIVIST MARTIN LUTHER KING JR.!!!~'

DEATHDAY # `-NUMBER = 1/30/20/06 = 1 + 30 + 20 + 06 = 57

(77 + 57) = 134 = (1 + 34) = 35 = RECIPROCAL = 53 = WAS `-MARRIED in (`-53)!!!~'

DWAYNE W. ANDERSON

BIRTH/DAY = 4/27 = (4 + 27) = 31 = DEATH/DAY = 1/30 = (1 + 30) = 31

BIRTH/MONTH = APRIL = 30 DAYS!!!~'

(30 (-) 27) – (DAY of BIRTH) = 3 = DEATH/DAY = 1/30 = (1 x 3 + 0) = 3

FRAGMENTED BIRTHDAY # `-NUMBER = 4 + 2 + 7 + 1 + 9 + 2 + 7 = 32

FRAGMENTED BIRTH/DAY # `-NUMBER = 32 = RECIPROCAL = 23 = "FLIP EVERY (`-2) OVER to a (`-7)"; "FLIP EVERY (`-3) OVER to an (`-8)" = 78 = AGE of DEATH for AMERICAN AUTHOR, ACTIVIST, CIVIL RIGHTS LEADER; AND, WIFE of MARTIN LUTHER KING JR. CORETTA SCOTT KING!!!~'

FRAGMENTED BIRTH/DAY # `-NUMBER = 32 = -a PROPHETIC # `-NUMBER!!!~'

FRAGMENTED BIRTH/DAY # `-NUMBER = 32 = FRAGMENTED `-DEATH/DAY of HUSBAND AMERICAN BAPTIST MINISTER AND ACTIVIST MARTIN LUTHER KING JR. = (`-32)!!!~'

FRAGMENTED DEATHDAY # `-NUMBER = 1 + 3 + 0 + 2 + 0 + 0 + 6 = 12

FRAGMENTED DEATH/DAY # `-NUMBER = 12 = (3 + 9) = AGE of DEATH for HUSBAND AMERICAN BAPTIST MINISTER AND ACTIVIST MARTIN LUTHER KING JR.!!!~'

(32 + 12) = 4/4 = DEATH/DAY of HUSBAND AMERICAN BAPTIST MINISTER AND ACTIVIST MARTIN LUTHER KING JR.!!!~'

(32 + 12) = (3 + 2) (1 + 2) = 53 = YEAR of `-MARRIAGE (`-53)!!!~'

DO '-YOU BELIEVE in '-GOD??? 'IS, '-DESTINY 'REAL???

WAS '-MARRIED to MARTIN LUTHER KING JR. from 1953 to 1968
= 15 YEARS = BIRTH/DAY of HUSBAND = 1/15 = (1 x 15) = 15!!!~'

'-MARRIED in (19/53) = (19 + 53) = 72 = RECIPROCAL = 27 =
(3 X 9) = AGE of DEATH for HUSBAND AMERICAN BAPTIST
MINISTER AND ACTIVIST MARTIN LUTHER KING JR.!!!~'

FROM BIRTH-TO-DEATH there are 87 DAYS = RECIPROCAL
= 78 = AGE of DEATH for AMERICAN AUTHOR, ACTIVIST,
CIVIL RIGHTS LEADER; AND, WIFE of MARTIN LUTHER
KING JR. CORETTA SCOTT KING!!!~'

(365 (-) 87) = 2(78) = (27 + 8) = 35 = RECIPROCAL = 53 = WAS
'-MARRIED in ('-53)!!!~'

CORETTA SCOTT KING was '-BORN in the '-MONTH of ('-4);
AND, '-DIED in the '-MONTH of ('-1) = 4/1 = DEATH/DAY #
'-NUMBER in '-REVERSE = (68 (-) 19 (-) 4 (-) 4) = ('-41) for HER
HUSBAND MARTIN LUTHER KING JR.!!!~'

HUSBAND MARTIN LUTHER KING JR..WAS '-BORN in the
'-MONTH of ('-1); AND, '-DIED in the '-MONTH of ('-4) = 1/4 =
RECIPROCAL = ('-41) = CORETTA SCOTT KING!!!~'

'-HUSBAND & '-WIFE were '-RECIPROCALS of '-EACH
'-OTHER!!!~'

AFRICAN-AMERICAN MUSLIM MINISTER AND HUMAN
RIGHTS ACTIVIST MALCOLM X died at the AGE of 39!!!~'

BIRTH/YEAR = 19/25 = (19 + 25) = 4/4 = DEATH/DAY of
AMERICAN BAPTIST MINISTER AND ACTIVIST MARTIN
LUTHER KING JR.!!!~'

DWAYNE W. ANDERSON

BIRTHDAY # `-NUMBER = 5/19/19/25 = 5 + 19 + 19 + 25 = 68

BIRTH/DAY # `-NUMBER = 68 = "FLIP EVERY (`-8) OVER to a (`-3)" = 63 = AGE of DEATH of WIFE AMERICAN EDUCATOR AND CIVIL RIGHTS ADVOCATE BETTY SHABAZZ!!!~'

DEATHDAY # `-NUMBER = 2/21/19/65 = 2 + 21 + 19 + 65 = 107

(107 (-) 68) = 39 = AGE of DEATH for AFRICAN-AMERICAN MUSLIM MINISTER AND HUMAN RIGHTS ACTIVIST MALCOLM X!!!~'

(107 + 68) = 175 = (1 – 7) (5) = 65 = DEATH/YEAR!!!~'

DAY of `-BIRTH = 19th = DEATH/DAY = 2/21 = (2 – 21) = 19

BIRTH/DAY = 5/19 = (5) (1 – 9) = 58 = WAS `-MARRIED in (`-58)!!!~'

BIRTH/DAY = 5/19 = (5 – 19) = 14 = (2 x 7) = 27 = (3 X 9) = AGE of DEATH for AFRICAN-AMERICAN MUSLIM MINISTER AND HUMAN RIGHTS ACTIVIST MALCOLM X!!!~'

DEATH/DAY = 2/21 = HALF RECIPROCAL = 2/12 = (2 + 12) = 14 = (2 x 7) = 27 = (3 X 9) = AGE of DEATH for AFRICAN-AMERICAN MUSLIM MINISTER AND HUMAN RIGHTS ACTIVIST MALCOLM X!!!~'

BIRTH/MONTH = MAY = 31 DAYS!!!~'

(31 (-) 19) – (DAY of BIRTH) = 12 = (3 + 9) = AGE of DEATH for AFRICAN-AMERICAN MUSLIM MINISTER AND HUMAN RIGHTS ACTIVIST MALCOLM X!!!~'

DAY of `-DEATH = 21st = RECIPROCAL = 12 = (3 + 9) = AGE of

DEATH for AFRICAN-AMERICAN MUSLIM MINISTER AND HUMAN RIGHTS ACTIVIST MALCOLM X!!!~'

DEATH/DAY = 2/21 = (2 + 21) = 23 = -a PROPHETIC # `-NUMBER!!!~'

DEATH/DAY # `-NUMBER in `-REVERSE = (65 (-) 19 (-) 21 (-) 2) = (`-23) = RECIPROCAL = (`-32) = FRAGMENTED BIRTH/DAY # `-NUMBER!!!~'

FRAGMENTED BIRTHDAY # `-NUMBER = 5 + 1 + 9 + 1 + 9 + 2 + 5 = 32

FRAGMENTED BIRTHDAY # `-NUMBER = 32 = -a PROPHETIC # `-NUMBER!!!~'

FRAGMENTED DEATHDAY # `-NUMBER = 2 + 2 + 1 + 1 + 9 + 6 + 5 = 26

(32 + 26) = 58 = WAS `-MARRIED in (`-58)!!!~'

DEATH/MONTH = FEBRUARY = 28 DAYS!!!~'

(28 (-) 21) – (DAY of `-DEATH) = 7 = WAS `-MARRIED for (`-7) YEARS!!!~'

WAS `-MARRIED to BETTY SHABAZZ from 1958 TO 1965 = 7 YEARS!!!~'

WAS `-MARRIED in (19 – 58) = 39 = AGE of DEATH for AFRICAN-AMERICAN MUSLIM MINISTER AND HUMAN RIGHTS ACTIVIST MALCOLM X!!!~'

FROM BIRTH-TO-DEATH there are 87 DAYS = RECIPROCAL = 78 / (DIVIDED by) (`-2) = 39 = AGE of DEATH for

DWAYNE W. ANDERSON

AFRICAN-AMERICAN MUSLIM MINISTER AND HUMAN RIGHTS ACTIVIST MALCOLM X!!!~'

FROM BIRTH-TO-DEATH there are 87 DAYS = (8 x 7) = 56 = RECIPROCAL = 65 = DEATH/YEAR!!!~'

FROM BIRTH-TO-DEATH there are 87 DAYS = (8 x 7) = 56 = BIRTH/DAY = 5/19 = "FLIP EVERY (`-9) OVER to a (`-6)" = 5/16 = (56 x 1) = 56!!!~'

(365 (-) 87) = 278 = (2 – 7) (8) = 58 = WAS `-MARRIED in (`-58) = BIRTH/DAY = 5/19 = (5) (1 – 9) = (`-58)!!!~'

WAS `-BORN in the `-MONTH of (`-5); AND, `-DIED in the `-MONTH (`-2) = 5/2 = RECIPROCAL = (`-25) = BIRTH/YEAR!!!~'

BIRTH/YEAR = 19/25 = (9) (1 x 2 – 5) = (9) (3) = 93 = RECIPROCAL = 39 = AGE of DEATH for AFRICAN-AMERICAN MUSLIM MINISTER AND HUMAN RIGHTS ACTIVIST MALCOLM X!!!~'

AMERICAN EDUCATOR AND CIVIL RIGHTS ADVOCATE BETTY SHABAZZ died at the AGE of 63!!!~'

DEATH/DAY # `-NUMBER in `-REVERSE = (97 (-) 19 (-) 23 (-) 6) = 49 = (4 x 9) = 36 = RECIPROCAL = 63 = AGE of DEATH for AMERICAN EDUCATOR AND CIVIL RIGHTS ADVOCATE BETTY SHABAZZ!!!~'

DEATH/YEAR = 19/97 = (19 – 97) = 78 = RECIPROCAL = 87 = DAYS from BIRTH-TO-DEATH for HUSBAND AFRICAN-AMERICAN MUSLIM MINISTER AND HUMAN RIGHTS ACTIVIST MALCOLM X!!!~'

DEATH/YEAR = 19/97 = (19 − 97) = 78 = (7 x 8) = 56 = WAS `-BORN in the `-MONTH of (`-5); AND, `-DIED in the `-MONTH of (`-6) = (`-56)!!!~'

BIRTH/DAY = 5/28 = HALF RECIPROCAL = 5/82 = (5 + 82) = 87 = DAYS from BIRTH-TO-DEATH for HUSBAND AFRICAN-AMERICAN MUSLIM MINISTER AND HUMAN RIGHTS ACTIVIST MALCOLM X!!!~'

BIRTH/DAY = 5/28 = (5) (2 − 8) = 56 = (7 x 8) = DEATH/YEAR = 19/97 = (19 − 97) = 78!!!~'

DEATH/DAY = 6/23 = (6) (2 + 3) = 65 = RECIPROCAL = 56 = (7 x 8) = DEATH/YEAR = 19/97 = (19 − 97) = 78!!!~'

BIRTHDAY # `-NUMBER = 5/28/19/34 = 5 + 28 + 19 + 34 = 86

BIRTH/DAY # `-NUMBER = 86 = RECIPROCAL = 68 = BIRTH/DAY # `-NUMBER of HUSBAND AFRICAN-AMERICAN MUSLIM MINISTER AND HUMAN RIGHTS ACTIVIST MALCOLM X!!!~'

BIRTH/DAY # `-NUMBER = 86 = RECIPROCAL = 68 = "FLIP EVERY (`-8) OVER to a (`-3)" = 63 = AGE of DEATH for AMERICAN EDUCATOR AND CIVIL RIGHTS ADVOCATE BETTY SHABAZZ!!!~'

BIRTH/DAY # `-NUMBER = 86 = (8 + 6) = 14 = (2 x 7) = 27 = (3 X 9) = AGE of DEATH for HUSBAND AFRICAN-AMERICAN MUSLIM MINISTER AND HUMAN RIGHTS ACTIVIST MALCOLM X!!!~'

DEATHDAY # `-NUMBER = 6/23/19/97 = 6 + 23 + 19 + 97 = 145

$(86 + 145) = 231 = (23 \times 1) = (\text{`-}23) = \text{-a PROPHETIC \# `-NUMBER} = \text{RECIPROCAL} = 32 = \text{FRAGMENTED BIRTH/DAY \# `-NUMBER!!!~'}$

$\text{BIRTH/DAY} = 5/28 = (5 - 28) = 23 = \text{DAY of `-DEATH} = (\text{`-}23)!!!~'$

$\text{DEATH/DAY} = 6/23 = (63 \times 2) = 126 = (1 \times 26) = 26 = \text{DAYS from BIRTH-TO-DEATH!!!~'}$

$\text{DEATH/DAY} = 6/23 = (6 + 23) = 29 = \text{"FLIP EVERY (`-9) OVER to a (`-6)"} = 26 = \text{DAYS from BIRTH-TO-DEATH!!!~'}$

$\text{FRAGMENTED BIRTHDAY \# `-NUMBER} = 5 + 2 + 8 + 1 + 9 + 3 + 4 = 32$

$\text{FRAGMENTED BIRTH/DAY \# `-NUMBER} = 32 = \text{-a PROPHETIC \# `-NUMBER!!!~'}$

$\text{FRAGMENTED BIRTH/DAY \# `-NUMBER} = 32 = \text{RECIPROCAL} = 23 = \text{DAY of `-DEATH!!!~'}$

$\text{FRAGMENTED DEATHDAY \# `-NUMBER} = 6 + 2 + 3 + 1 + 9 + 9 + 7 = 37$

$\text{FRAGMENTED DEATH/DAY \# `-NUMBER} = 37 = \text{"FLIP EVERY (`-7) OVER to a (`-2)"} = 32 = \text{FRAGMENTED BIRTH/DAY \# `-NUMBER} = (\text{`-}32)!!!~'$

$\text{FRAGMENTED BIRTH/DAY \# `-NUMBER} = (\text{`-}32) = \text{FRAGMENTED `-BIRTH/DAY \# `-NUMBER of `-HUSBAND AFRICAN-AMERICAN MUSLIM MINISTER AND HUMAN RIGHTS ACTIVIST MALCOLM X} = (\text{`-}32)!!!~'$

$(32 + 32) = 64 = \text{RECIPROCAL} = 46 = (19 - 65) = \text{DEATH/YEAR of `-HUSBAND AFRICAN-AMERICAN MUSLIM MINISTER AND HUMAN RIGHTS ACTIVIST MALCOLM X!!!~'}$

DEATH/MONTH = JUNE = 30 DAYS!!!~'

(30 (-) 23) – (DAY of '-DEATH) = 7 = WAS '-MARRIED for ('-7) YEARS!!!~'

WAS '-MARRIED to MALCOLM X from 1958 TO 1965 = 7 YEARS!!!~'

WAS '-MARRIED in (19 – 58) = 39 = AGE of DEATH for '-HER '-HUSBAND AFRICAN-AMERICAN MUSLIM MINISTER AND HUMAN RIGHTS ACTIVIST MALCOLM X!!!~'

BIRTH/YEAR = 19/34 = (19 + 34) = 53 = "FLIP EVERY ('-3) OVER to an ('-8)" = 58 = YEAR '-MARRIED!!!~'

FROM BIRTH-TO-DEATH there are 26 DAYS = RECIPROCAL = 62 = "FLIP EVERY ('-6) OVER to a ('-9)"; "FLIP EVERY ('- 2) OVER to a ('-7)" = 97 = DEATH/YEAR!!!~'

(365 (-) 26) = 3(39) = (3 – 39) = 36 = RECIPROCAL = 63 = AGE of DEATH for AMERICAN EDUCATOR AND CIVIL RIGHTS ADVOCATE BETTY SHABAZZ!!!~'

FORMER FIRST LADY MARY ANN TODD LINCOLN died at the AGE of 63!!!~'

WAS '-BORN in the '-MONTH of ('-12); AND, '-DIED in the '-MONTH of ('-7) = 12/7 = RECIPROCAL = 7/12 = "FLIP EVERY ('-7) OVER to a ('-2)" = 2/12 = HUSBAND'S BIRTHDAY #16/PRESIDENT OF THE UNITED STATES OF AMERICA ABRAHAM LINCOLN!!!~'

BIRTH/YEAR = 18/18 = (18 + 18) = 36 = RECIPROCAL = 63 =

AGE of DEATH for FORMER FIRST LADY MARY ANN TODD LINCOLN!!!~'

BIRTHDAY # `-NUMBER = 12/13/18/18 = 12 + 13 + 18 + 18 = 61

BIRTH/DAY # `-NUMBER = 61 = RECIPROCAL = 16 = DAY of `-DEATH!!!~'

DEATH/DAY = 7/16 = (7 + 16) = 23 = -a PROPHETIC # `-NUMBER!!!~'

DEATHDAY # `-NUMBER = 7/16/18/82 = 7 + 16 + 18 + 82 = 123

(61 + 123) = 184 = (1 – 84) = 83 = YEAR `-MARRIAGE `-ENDED = (18 + 65) = 83

DEATH/DAY # `-NUMBER = 123 = (1 x 23) = 23 = -a PROPHETIC # `-NUMBER!!!~'

DEATH/DAY # `-NUMBER in `-REVERSE = (82 (-) 18 (-) 16 (-) 7) = 41 = BIRTH/DAY # `-NUMBER of `-HUSBAND #16/ PRESIDENT OF THE UNITED STATES OF AMERICA ABRAHAM LINCOLN!!!~'

FRAGMENTED BIRTHDAY # `-NUMBER = 1 + 2 + 1 + 3 + 1 + 8 + 1 + 8 = 25

FRAGMENTED BIRTH/DAY # `-NUMBER = 25 = BIRTH/DAY = 12/13 = (12 + 13) = 25

FRAGMENTED BIRTH/DAY # `-NUMBER = 25 = RECIPROCAL = 52 = HEIGHT = 5' 2"!!!~'

FRAGMENTED DEATHDAY # `-NUMBER = 7 + 1 + 6 + 1 + 8 + 8 + 2 = 33

$(25 + 33) = 58 =$ "FLIP EVERY (`-8) OVER to a (`-3)" $= 53 = \#$ `-NUMBERS of `-HUSBAND #16/ PRESIDENT OF THE UNITED STATES OF AMERICA ABRAHAM LINCOLN!!!~'

$(25 + 33) = (2 + 5) (3 \times 3) = (`-79) = (7 \times 9) = 63 =$ AGE of DEATH for FORMER FIRST LADY MARY ANN TODD LINCOLN!!!~'

BIRTH/MONTH = DECEMBER = 31 DAYS!!!~'

$(31 (-) 13) -$ (DAY of BIRTH) $= 18 =$ BIRTH/YEAR $= 18 = (6 \times 3) =$ AGE of DEATH for FORMER FIRST LADY MARY ANN TODD LINCOLN!!!~'

WAS `-MARRIED to #16 PRESIDENT ABRAHAM LINCOLN from 1842 to 1865 = 23 YEARS = "FLIP EVERY (`-2) OVER to a (`-7)"; "FLIP EVERY (`-3) OVER to an (`-8)" $= 78 = (7 + 8) = 15 =$ "SEE `-BELOW" $= (7 \times 8) = (`-56) =$ AGE of DEATH for HUSBAND #16/ PRESIDENT OF THE UNITED STATES OF AMERICA ABRAHAM LINCOLN!!!~'

DEATH/MONTH = JULY = 31 DAYS!!!~'

$(31 (-) 16) -$ (DAY of DEATH) $= 15 =$ DAYS from BIRTH-TO-DEATH $= 150 = (15 + 0) = 15!!!~'$

FROM BIRTH-TO-DEATH there are 150 DAYS $= (15 + 0) = 15 =$ "SEE `-ABOVE"!!!~'

$(365 (-) 150) = 215 = (25 \times 1) = 25 =$ FRAGMENTED BIRTH/DAY # `-NUMBER = RECIPROCAL $= 5/2 = 5' 2" =$ HEIGHT!!!~'

BIRTH/YEAR $= 18/18 = (1 + 8 + 1 + 8) = 18 = (6 \times 3) =$ AGE of DEATH for FORMER FIRST LADY MARY ANN TODD LINCOLN!!!~'

DEATH/YEAR = 18/82 = (1 x 8) (8 – 2) = 86 = RECIPROCAL = 68 = "FLIP EVERY (`-8) OVER to a (`-3)" = 63 = AGE of DEATH for FORMER FIRST LADY MARY ANN TODD LINCOLN!!!~'

#16/PRESIDENT OF THE UNITED STATES OF AMERICA ABRAHAM LINCOLN died at the AGE of 56!!!~'

BIRTHDAY # `-NUMBER = 2/12/18/09 = 2 + 12 + 18 + 09 = 41

BIRTH/DAY # `-NUMBER = 41 = FIRST `-PART of DEATH/DAY = (41)5!!!~'

DEATHDAY # `-NUMBER = 4/15/18/65 = 4 + 15 + 18 + 65 = 102

DEATH/DAY # `-NUMBER in `-REVERSE = (65 (-) 18 (-) 15 (-) 4) = 28 = BIRTH/DAY = 2/12 = "FLIP EVERY (`-2) OVER to a (`-7)" = 2/17 = (2) (1 + 7) = 28

(28 + 28) = 56 = AGE of DEATH for #16/PRESIDENT OF THE UNITED STATES OF AMERICA ABRAHAM LINCOLN!!!~'

(102 (-) 41) = 61 = BIRTHDAY # `-NUMBER (`-61) of WIFE FORMER FIRST LADY MARY ANN TODD LINCOLN = RECIPROCAL = 16 = PRESIDENTIAL # `-NUMBER = 16!!!~'

BIRTH/DAY = 2/12 = HALF RECIPROCAL = 2/21 = (2 + 21) = 23 = -a PROPHETIC # `-NUMBER!!!~'

BIRTH/DAY = 2/12 = HALF RECIPROCAL = 2/21 = (2 x 21) = 42 /|\ (42 + 23) = 65 = DEATH/YEAR = RECIPROCAL = 56 = AGE of DEATH for #16/PRESIDENT OF THE UNITED STATES OF AMERICA ABRAHAM LINCOLN!!!~'

PART of BIRTH = (2 + 12 + 18) = 32 = -a PROPHETIC # '-NUMBER!!!~'

BIRTH/MONTH = FEBRUARY = 28 DAYS!!!~

(28 (-) 12) – (DAY of BIRTH) = 16 = RECIPROCAL = 61 = "SEE '-ABOVE"!!!~'

DEATH/DAY = 4/15 = (4) (1 + 5) = 46 = AGE of '-WIFE FORMER FIRST LADY MARY ANN TODD LINCOLN at TIME of '-HER '-HUSBAND'S ASSASSINATION = RECIPROCAL = 64 = WIFE'S DEATH/YEAR = (18 – 82) = ('-64)!!!~'

DEATH/YEAR = 18/65 = (1 + 8 – 5) (6) = 46 = AGE of '-WIFE FORMER FIRST LADY MARY ANN TODD LINCOLN at TIME of '-HER '-HUSBAND'S ASSASSINATION = RECIPROCAL = 64 = WIFE'S DEATH/YEAR = (18 – 82) = ('-64)!!!~'

DEATH/DAY = 4/15 = (4) (1 + 5) = 46 = RECIPROCAL = 64 = HEIGHT = 6' 4"!!!~'

FRAGMENTED BIRTHDAY # '-NUMBER = 2 + 1 + 2 + 1 + 8 + 0 + 9 = 23

FRAGMENTED BIRTH/DAY # '-NUMBER = 23 = -a PROPHETIC # '-NUMBER!!!~'

FRAGMENTED BIRTH/DAY # '-NUMBER = 23 = YEARS '-MARRIED = ('-23)!!!~'

FRAGMENTED DEATHDAY # '-NUMBER = 4 + 1 + 5 + 1 + 8 + 6 + 5 = 30

FRAGMENTED DEATH/DAY # '-NUMBER = 30 = (5 X 6) = AGE of DEATH for #16/PRESIDENT OF THE UNITED STATES OF AMERICA ABRAHAM LINCOLN!!!~'

(23 + 30) = 53 = "FLIP EVERY (`-3) OVER to an (`-8)" = 58 = # `-NUMBERS of `-WIFE FORMER FIRST LADY MARY ANN TODD LINCOLN!!!~'

WAS `-MARRIED to MARY TODD LINCOLN from 1842 TO 1865 = 23 YEARS = "FLIP EVERY (`-2) OVER to a (`-7)"; "FLIP EVERY (`-3) OVER to an (`-8)" = 78 = (7 x 8) = (`-56) = AGE of DEATH for #16/PRESIDENT OF THE UNITED STATES OF AMERICA ABRAHAM LINCOLN!!!~'

FROM BIRTH-TO-DEATH there are 62 DAYS = (6 x 2) = 12 = DAY of `-BIRTH = (12th)!!!~'

(365 (-) 62) = 303 = (30 + 3) = 33 / (DIVIDED by) (`-2) = 16.5 = ROUNDED DOWN = 16

(365 (-) 62) = 303 = (30 + 3) = 33 = FRAGMENTED `-DEATH/DAY # `-NUMBER of WIFE FORMER FIRST LADY MARY ANN TODD LINCOLN!!!~'

PRESIDENTIAL TERM `-STARTED on (3/4) 18/61!!!~'

(3 + 4 + 18 + 61) = 86 = RECIPROCAL = 68 = "FLIP EVERY (`-8) OVER to a (`-3)" = 63 = AGE of `-DEATH of `-WIFE FORMER FIRST LADY MARY ANN TODD LINCOLN!!!~'

(18/61) = (18 + 61) = 79 = (7 x 9) = 63 = AGE of `-DEATH of `-WIFE FORMER FIRST LADY MARY ANN TODD LINCOLN!!!~'

DEATH/DAY = 4/15 = (4 – 15) = 11 = (5 + 6) = 56 = AGE of DEATH for #16/PRESIDENT OF THE UNITED STATES OF AMERICA ABRAHAM LINCOLN!!!~'

DEATH/YEAR = 65 = RECIPROCAL = 56 = AGE of DEATH for #16/PRESIDENT OF THE UNITED STATES OF AMERICA ABRAHAM LINCOLN!!!~'

DEATH/YEAR = 18/65 = (1 + 8 + 5) (6) = (14) (6) = (1 x 4) (6) = 46 = RECIPROCAL = 64 = "SEE `-ABOVE" FOR WIFE (DEATH/ YEAR 18 – 82) FORMER FIRST LADY MARY ANN TODD LINCOLN = HEIGHT = 6' 4" of #16/PRESIDENT OF THE UNITED STATES OF AMERICA ABRAHAM LINCOLN!!!~'

BIRTH/YEAR = 18/09 = (1 x 8) (0 + 9) = 89 = RECIPROCAL = 98 = "FLIP EVERY (`-9) OVER to a (`-6)"; "FLIP EVERY (`-8) OVER to a (`-3)" = 63 = AGE of `-DEATH of `-WIFE FORMER FIRST LADY MARY ANN TODD LINCOLN!!!~'

AMERICAN PROFESSIONAL BOXER AND ACTIVIST MUHAMMAD ALI died at the AGE of 74!!!~'

BIRTHDAY # `-NUMBER = 1/17/19/42 = 1 + 17 + 19 + 42 = 79

BIRTHDAY # `-NUMBER = 79 = (7 x 9) = 6/3 = DEATH/DAY!!!~'

BIRTHDAY # `-NUMBER = 79 = (7 x 9) = 63 = RECIPROCAL = 36 = DEATH/YEAR = (20 + 16) = (`-36)!!!~'

DEATHDAY # `-NUMBER = 6/3/20/16 = 6 + 3 + 20 + 16 = 45

(79 + 45) = 124 = (1 – 24) = 23 = -a PROPHETIC # `-NUMBER!!!~'

BIRTH/YEAR = 19/42 = (19 – 42) = 23 = -a PROPHETIC # `-NUMBER!!!~'

DEATH/YEAR = 20/16 = (20 + 16) = 36 = RECIPROCAL = 6/3 = DEATH/DAY!!!~'

BIRTH/DAY = 1/17 = (1 + 17) = 18 = (6 X 3) = DEATH/DAY!!!~'

BIRTH/MONTH = JANUARY = 31 DAYS!!!~'

(31 (-) 17) – (DAY of BIRTH) = 14 = ($\underline{2}$ X $\underline{7}$)!!!~'

DEATH/MONTH = JUNE = 30 DAYS!!!~'

(30 (-) 3) – (DAY of DEATH) = (`-$\underline{27}$)!!!~'

(27 + 27) = 54 = RECIPROCAL = 45 = DEATH/DAY # `-NUMBER!!!~'

FRAGMENTED BIRTHDAY # `-NUMBER = 1 + 1 + 7 + 1 + 9 + 4 + 2 = 25

FRAGMENTED DEATHDAY # `-NUMBER = 6 + 3 + 2 + 0 + 1 + 6 = 18

FRAGMENTED DEATH/DAY # `-NUMBER = 18 = (6 X 3) = DEATH/DAY!!!~'

HEIGHT 6' 3" = DEATH/DAY = 6/3!!!~'

(25 + 18) = (2 + 5) (1 + 8) = 79 = (7 x 9) = 6/3 = DEATH/DAY!!!~'

PART of BIRTH/DAY = (1 + 17 + 19) = (`-37)!!!~'

FROM BIRTH-TO-DEATH there are 137 DAYS = RECIPROCAL = 731 = (73 + 1) = 74 = AGE of DEATH for AMERICAN PROFESSIONAL BOXER AND ACTIVIST MUHAMMAD ALI!!!~'

(365 (-) 137) = 228 = (22 – 8) = 14 = (2 x 7) = BIRTH/DAY = 1/17 = (1 + 1) (7) = (`-27)!!!~'

WAS `-BORN in the `-MONTH of (`-1); AND, `-DIED in the `-MONTH of (`-6) = 1/6 = DEATH/YEAR = (`-16)!!!~'

BIRTH/YEAR = 19/42 = (19 + 42) = 61 = RECIPROCAL = 16 = DEATH/YEAR!!!~'

BIRTH/YEAR = 19/42 = (1 x 4) (9 – 2) = 47 = RECIPROCAL = 74 = AGE of DEATH for AMERICAN PROFESSIONAL BOXER AND ACTIVIST MUHAMMAD ALI!!!~'

BIRTH/YEAR = 42 = "FLIP EVERY (`-2) OVER to a (`-7)" = 47 = RECIPROCAL = 74 = AGE of DEATH for AMERICAN PROFESSIONAL BOXER AND ACTIVIST MUHAMMAD ALI!!!~

DO `-YOU BELIEVE in `-GOD???

'IS, `-DESTINY 'REAL???

AUTHOR: MR. DWAYNE W. ANDERSON!!!~'

THE `-END /|\

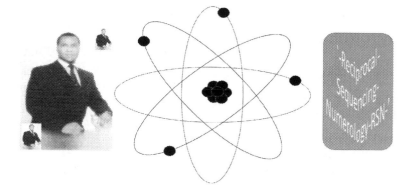

A HAUNTING DISCOVERY!!!~'

DENY the PATTERNS!!!~'

"DO YOU BELIEVE in GOD??? IS DESTINY REAL???" AUTHOR: DWAYNE W. ANDERSON!~

The ADDAMS FAMILY CAROLYN SUE JONES (HER FIRST MARRIAGE to AARON SPELLING was in 53) SHE died AT AGE 53! SHE DIVORCED AARON SPELLING in 1964 = 19+64 = 83 and SHE died in the YEAR of 83! Within MY NEW BOOK: "DO YOU BELIEVE in GOD??? IS DESTINY REAL???" AUTHOR: DWAYNE W. ANDERSON!~

The ADDAMS FAMILY LURCH THEODORE CRAWFORD CASSIDY (FRAG BIRTH # NUMBER 7+3+1+1+9+3+2 = 26 = FLIP EVERY 2 to 7; FLIP EVERY 6 to 9 = 79 = DEATHYEAR! 26 = RECIP = 62 = 92 / 2 = 46 = AGE of DEATH! MY NEW BOOK: "DO YOU BELIEVE in GOD??? IS DESTINY REAL???" AUTHOR: DWAYNE W. ANDERSON!~

AMERICAN SINGER & CO-FOUNDER of MUSICAL GROUP "FOUNTAINS of `-WAYNE" ADAM SCHLESINGER died at the AGE of (`-52) (BIRTH: 10/ 31/1967) (DEATH: 4/1/2020)!~' BIRTHDAY = 10+31 = 4/1 = DEATH/DAY!~' BIRTH/YEAR 1/9/6/7 = 1-6/9-7 = 52 = AGE of DEATH!!!~' /|\ BOOK TITLE: `-GOD is `-the MATHEMATICIAN-`"!!!~' /|\

NIKOLA TESLA (AC) had a BIRTHDAY of (7/10) = 7 + 10 = 17 = HIS DEATH/DAY (JAN. 7TH)!!!~' AMERICAN SINGER & CO-FOUNDER of MUSICAL GROUP "FOUNTAINS of `-WAYNE" ADAM SCHLESINGER had a BIRTHDAY of (10/31) = 10 + 31 = 4/1 = (APRIL 1ST) = DEATH/DAY!!!~' THESE' are NOT UNIQUE PATTERNS!!!~'

STAR WARS' ALAN WALBRIDGE LADD, JR died at the AGE of 84 = (8 x 4) = 32 = DEATH/DAY!!!~' HE died on 3/2 = MARCH 2nd!!!~' HIS '-BIRTHDAY was 10/22 = (10 + 22) = 32 = DEATH/ DAY!!!~' FROM BIRTH-TO-DEATH = 131 DAYS = (1 + 31) = 32 = DEATH/DAY!!!~' BORN in 1937 = (1-9) (3-7) = 84 = AGE of DEATH!!!~' DEATH/YEAR = 20/22 = (20 + 22) = 42 (x 2) = 84 = AGE of DEATH!!!~'

FIRST FEMALE SECRETARY of STATE in U.S. HISTORY MADELEINE JANA KORBEL ALBRIGHT came to AMERICA in 48 = RECIPROCAL = 84 = AGE of DEATH!~' BIRTH = 5+15+19+37 = 76 = 7x6 = 42 (x 2) = 84!~' DEATH = 3+23+20+22 = 68 = 6 x 8 = 48 = RECIPROCAL = 84!~ BIRTH/YEAR = 1937 = 1-9 / 3-7 = 84 = AGE of DEATH!~'

FIRST FEMALE SECRETARY of STATE in U.S. HISTORY MADELEINE JANA KORBEL ALBRIGHT came to AMERICA in 48 = RECIPROCAL = 84 = AGE of DEATH = 84 = 8x4 = 32 = DEATH/DAY = 3/23 = 3+2 / 3 = 53 = DAYS from BIRTH-to-DEATH!~' (365 (-) 53) = 312 = 32x1 = 32 = 8x4 = AGE of DEATH!~' BIRTHDAY # = 76 = 7x6 = 42 = DEATH/YEAR = 20+22 = 42!~'

FOOTBALL PLAYER DWAYNE HASKINS JR. died TODAY at the AGE of 24 that was 24 DAYS AWAY from BIRTHDAY to DEATHDAY!~" HIS BIRTHDAY # = 5+3+19+97 = 124 = 1X24 = 24!~' 124 = 12x4 = 48 = DIED the VERY NEXT DAY on 4/9!~' BIRTHYEAR = 9x7 = 63 = RECIP = 36 = 4x9 = DEATHDAY!!!~'

SENATOR ORRIN GRANT HATCH died 32 DAYS after HIS last BIRTHDAY of 3/22 on THE 23rd DAY of APRIL!~' BIRTH = 32x2 = 64 = 8x8 = AGE of DEATH!~' HEIGHT = 6' 2" = RECIP = 26 = (62 + 26) = 88 = AGE of DEATH!~' FRAG BIRTH # = 3+2+2+1+9+3+4 = 24 = RECIP = 42 YEARS as SENATOR = 20+22 = 42 = DEATHYEAR!~'

SENATOR ORRIN GRANT HATCH died ON a 23rd; 32 DAYS from HIS LAST BIRTHDAY of (3/2)2!~' BIRTHDAY # = 3+22+19+34 = 78 = RECIP = 87 = DIED 32 DAYS from 87 = FLIP 8,7 = 3,2!~' 1934 = 1-9/3+4 = 87!~' MARRIED on 8(2)8 in 19+57 = 76 = WAS FIRST ELECTED in 19(76) = 7x6 = 42 = SERVED 42 YEARS in the SENATE!~

JEFF GLADNEY was an AMERICAN FOOTBALL (CB) BIRTHDAY # in REVERSE = 96-19-12-12 = 53 = DEATH/DAY = 5/30 = 5+30 = 35 = RECIP = 53!!!~' AMERICAN RAPPER CHYNNA ROGERS'-REVERSE on '-HER '-BIRTHDAY # = (94-19-19-8) = 48 = HER VERY OWN '-DEATH/DAY = APRIL 8th!!!~' A COMMON PATTERN!!!~'

OIL TYCOON T. BOONE PICKENS DIED at 91 & was BORN in 1928 = 9(1+2+8) = 911 = HIS DEATHDAY & AGE of DEATH = 911!~' AMERICAN SINGER/SONGWRITER EDDIE MONEY died at the AGE of 70 & was MARRIED to HIS WIFE LAURIE MONEY IN 1989 = 19(-)89 = ('-70) = AGE of DEATH = /|\ REGULAR PATTERNS!~

PLAYBOY'S HUGH HEFNER'S '-BIRTHDAY = (4/9/1926) & HE DIED at the AGE of (91)!~' TAKE the 1 from 1926; and, ADD IT to 926 = 926 + 1 = 927 = SEPTEMBER 27th = DEATHDAY!~' OIL TYCOON T. BOONE PICKENS DIED at 91 & was BORN in 1928 = 9(1+2+8) = 911 = HIS DEATHDAY & AGE of DEATH = 911~'

ACTOR PHILIP BAKER HALL dies at 90 years of age (90) days away from his BIRTHDAY!~' BIRTHDAY = 9/10 = 9x10 = 90!~' DEATHDAY 6+12+20+22 = 60 = 6 to 9 = 90!~' BIRTHDAY # = 9+10+19+31 = 69 = DIED in the MONTH of 6 & was BORN in the MONTH of 9!~' 'WAKE UP!!! to the PATTERNS '-PEOPLE!!!~'

CANADIAN TELEVISION ACTRESS SHIRLEY DOUGLAS DIED at 86 (BIRTH: APRIL 2, 1934) (DEATH: APRIL 5, 2020)!~' BIRTHYEAR = 34x2 = 68 = RECIP = 86 = AGE of DEATH!~'`-BIRTHDAY # '-NUMBER = 4+2+19+34 = 59 = 5x9 = 4/5 = DAY of DEATH!~' ALL of the FAMILY is INTERCONNECTED as ALL the REST of US!~'

FOOTBALL PLAYER BOBBY CORNELIUS MITCHELL DEATH 84 (BIRTH: 6/6, 1935) (DEATH: 4/5, 2020)!~' BIRTHYEAR = 1935 = 19+35 = 54 = RECIP = 45 = DAY of DEATH!~' ENTREPRENEUR EARL G. GRAVES, SR. DEATH 85 (BIRTH: 1/9, 1935) (DEATH: 4/6, 2020)!~' BIRTHDAY # = (1+9+19+35) = 64 = RECIP = 46 = DAY of DEATH!~'

PBS NEWSHOUR/CNN'S MARK STEPHEN SHIELDS dies TODAY at the AGE of 85 = BIRTHDAY # = 5+25+19+37 = 86 = RECIP = 68 = DEATH/DAY = 6/18 = 68x1 = 68!~' 6+18 = 24 = DIED 24 DAYS after BIRTHDAY!~' CHECK MY TWITTER @ thebrspider!~' This PATTERN is for EVERYONE!~' @CNN @ CNNBRK @JudyWoodruff

AMERICAN ACTOR RAYMOND THOMAS BAILEY "CHARACTER = WEALTHY BANKER MILBURN DRYSDALE of THE BEVERLY HILLBILLIES" died at the AGE of 75!~' FRAG BIRTHDAY # = 5+6+1+9+0+4 = 25 = FLIP 2 to 7 = 75 = AGE of DEATH!~' BIRTHYEAR = 1904 = 19x4 = 76 = DIED within HIS 76th YEAR of EXISTENCE!~' BIRTHDAY = 5/6 = 5x6 = 30 = FLIP 3 to 8 = 80 = DEATH/YEAR!~' BIRTHDAY # = 5+6+19+04 = 34 = FLIP 3 to 8 = 84 / (DIVIDED by) ('-2) = 42!!!~' DEATHDAY # in REVERSE = 80(-)19(-)15(-)4 = 42!!!~' FRAG DEATHDAY # = 4+1+5+1+9+8+0 = 28 (X TIMES) ('-2) = 56 = BIRTH/DAY!!!~' BIRTHYEAR = 1904 = 19(04) = 19(-)4 = 15 = (4/15) = DEATH/DAY!!!~'

I had FORGOTTEN to INCLUDE MR. BAILEY in ONE of MY NEW BOOKS: "The `-GOD `-BOOK of `-NUMEROLOGY!~'" as I had INCLUDED ALL of the OTHER CHARACTERS of the BEVERLY HILLBILLIES SHOW!!!~'

The WORLD is IN /|\ for a RUDE AWAKENING!!!~'

'-/|\ - /|\ - /|\ - /|\ - /|\ -'

The "PROPHET": DWAYNE W. ANDERSON!!!~'